India
Contemporary

India
Contemporary

Henry Wilson

Thames & Hudson

To Dr John
For love, consideration
and companionship

First published in 2007 in hardcover in the United
States of America by Thames & Hudson Inc.,
500 Fifth Avenue, New York, New York 10110

thamesandhudsonusa.com

Library of Congress Catalog Card Number:
2006940568

ISBN 978-0-500-51365-1

Printed and bound in Singapore
by CS Graphics Pte Limited

on the half-title page
Glass bangles adapted as vases in the house
of Lakha and Anupam Poddar (see p. 151).

on the title page
In a Delhi courtyard house billowing fabric catches
the breeze. The door in the background displays
Raseel Gujral Ansal's signature weave motif. The
shapely table gives a sexy edge to the composition.

opposite
An interior by Raseel Gujral Ansal in a house in
New Delhi conceived by her father, the painter,
sculptor and architect Satish Gujral. A teardrop
vessel stands on a pedestal where the staircase
divides. We are looking into the region used by the
clients' son: a chill-out zone, between a bar area
on one side and a disco floor on the other.

pages 6–7
The austere and dramatic dining area in the house
of Raj and Dinesh Himatsingka (see pp. 134–39).
The lamps are precisely positioned across the
recess, offset by a bank of flowers, and the organic
flow of the Persian rug is held in by its strict outline.

pages 8–9
Detail of a carved wooden overdoor from one
of the grand 19th-century mansions of the
Nattukottai Chettiars, a mercantile community
in Chettinad district, Tamil Nadu, placed in a new
Indian context by the Frenchman Dimitri Klein.

page 11

upper left square
top left Dramatic spiral forms in Nirmala
Rudhra's apartment (see pp. 72–73).
top right Plates from Sonali Purewal's 'Akshar'
collection, sold in her store, Zen Space, in Delhi.
bottom left Porcelain from Michael Aram's 'Lotus'
collection, and pepper and salt shakers by him,
in his apartment (see p. 108).
bottom right A South Indian pot, painted by
Carol Arnaud-Goddet (see pp. 112–13).
upper right square
A bronze statue of Krishna as a playful child
rests on an antique fabric from Gujarat, in
Satish Gupta's house (p. 32).
lower left square
Detail of the mural in the entrance to Rajshree
Pathy's house (see p. 61): Krishna as 'Kalki', on
horseback, during his last appearance on earth.
lower right square
A collage of fabrics used by Raseel Gujral Ansal.

page 12

left A wall covered with bronze tiles, in a project
by Rajiv Saini; against them, in stark relief, is a
bronze tree with leaves cast by the traditional lost-
wax technique.
right Naïve papier-mâché busts of Hindu deities,
presented to Rachel and Pritam Singh of Jaipur.

page 13

left A plaster relief in Mughal style, in the New
Delhi garden of the connoisseur Romi Chopra.
right A contemporary sculpture by Rathore,
in the home of Tarun Tahiliani (see p. 183).

The drawings used as vignettes are by Henry Wilson.

Introduction

In February 2006 the Indian paper *Tehelka* blazed on its front cover: 'What's Right about India – Vibrant. Resilient. Resurgent. Ancient. Rooted. Inclusive. Plural. Singular – Country Unputdownable.' India has entered an extraordinary period, the most exciting since independence in 1947.

India is now the world's fastest-growing free-market democracy. In 2005 there were over 23 million new mobile phone users and 40 new models of cars; in 2006 India placed orders for more than two hundred new jetliners and the single biggest order on record for aero engines. The 'Golden Quadrilateral' highway, 6,000 kilometres long, is projected to link the four biggest cities, Delhi, Mumbai, Chennai and Kolkata (Bombay, Madras and Calcutta to old-timers). The arrival of the likes of Cartier and Chanel, with swanky new boutiques, has changed the shopping experience out of all recognition. More than 4,000 major multinationals are investing in the country, while many more are circling like bees round the honey pot.

India has gone global and there's a rush to be part of it. Banished are the hackneyed images of a poor, post-colonial subcontinent. This is a modern country with a youthful voice that we increasingly must listen to – and not just through a call centre! Today, India shows off a culture informed by its past but transcending it, making it an exciting contemporary influence on our lives. 'New Indian chic' is everywhere: cuisine, fashion, music, film, travel destination, not to mention the new wellbeing lifestyles, yoga and Ayurveda.

Certain of their own tradition and heritage, Indians can pick and choose from their own cultural storeroom, and experiment by combining its contents with creative concepts from the rest of the world. Such a point in the country's history is a fascinating moment in which to explore India's homes and their design and decoration. It is a vast subject. This in itself is an excellent reflection of the country's heightened, eclective creative spirit, ranging from historical to contemporary, from preservation and restoration to creating for the future.

The tradition of communal living and the extended family is in decline, particularly in the urban context, replaced by the nuclear family and single-occupancy apartments. With burgeoning incomes, Indians are travelling in numbers which could not have been anticipated even a few years ago, and India is being influenced by styles from Thailand and Singapore, its local neighbours, as well as from much further afield.

For captions, see p. 4

An expanding contingent of Indians in the creative fields are sourcing their inspiration locally and internationally. For years this new movement was hamstrung by the lack of patrons or a commercial market. Now the designers have the necessary encouragement, through the new national wealth and the hungry global market. Their vision has filtered through both to the Indian home and increasingly abroad, too.

India has exported physical labour and, more recently, intellectual, scientific and medical expertise to the world. Unexpectedly, there is now a counter-flow. Anxious to be a part of the meteoric rise of the mother country, people of Indian origin are returning, and inspiring those around them with their imported styles and tastes. Foreigners too are flowing in to meet the various new demands. Artists and designers are bringing their Western creativity, and also merging with it the culture and styles that surround them, taking advantage of India's extraordinary wealth of skilled artisans and arriving at new and imaginative ideas and products.

Indian homes reflect the subcontinent's geographic and climatic differences – the subalpine Himalayan foothills, the subtropical far south, the desert-like west, and the vast enveloping coastline. And then there

For captions, see p. 4

are the strong religious influences and sensibilities which continue to have a bearing on the family home.

It is not only the country's wealthiest families who are driving the forces of change, but the vast middle class, who as the writer Pavan Varma put it in *Tehelka* 'are harmonious schizophrenics': 'The middle class mind is not a cupboard. It is a chest of drawers. Pull out one drawer and you find the middle class person's fingers on a keyboard in tandem with the change in the 21st century. Pull out another and it is responding to some obscurantist impulse which predates the computer by 2,000 years. . . . For civilizations as old as ours where one cannot get rid of the past very easily, the ability to allow more than one time zone to coexist within oneself is a tremendous strength. In most countries, people would be paralysed by the sheer contradiction of it. But not the Indian middle class.' The *puja* room, the family prayer space, coexists with Gucci furnishings.

At few other points in its history has India had such a tangible and binding sense of collective destiny. This heady feeling was recently encapsulated in the slogan 'India Shining'. Even those who dismissed that as spin could not have imagined how true the image would turn out to be: international acknowledgment is matched at home with provable fact. The shine has never seemed so bright.

A hallway leading to guest bedrooms in the house of Manju and Sonali Purewal in the foothills of the Himalayas. For the couple, the surrounding environment was a crucial consideration when it came to building their new family home. Set on a craggy outcrop, it exploits its position through the use of huge plate-glass panes for its walls: you seem almost to be able to reach out and touch the forest.

Future Present

India today has an advantage which few other countries in the world possess: the ability to dream in more than one language. It can pick from its own rich tradition and culture and at the same time from the Western psyche through long association. And like the West, India has never been (metaphorically speaking) regimented, unlike its major competitor, China: it is a country of the individual rather than the collective.

India has always had the capacity to tolerate and assimilate both aggressive and passive visitors. Over the last thousand years these have included Muslims, Christians (in the form of the French, Portuguese and British, and before them the Syrian Christians), Jews, Parsis from Iran, and the invading hippies of the 1960s. And in spite of its diversity, India has enjoyed a period of cultural unity longer than that of any other society, unified both as a state of mind and physically through its indigenous religion and its sacred sites that cover its subcontinental peninsula like a fine cobweb.

This is particularly true of architecture: the Mughal language was taken up by the Rajputs; the Victorian style from Britain took on a local flavour to become 'Indo-Saracenic'. More recently, with considerable verve, India adopted Art Deco, perhaps the first pan-global style. Even the State was prepared to experiment with the avant-garde when, in the 1950s, it invited Le Corbusier to design the new city of Chandigarh. More recent times have seen the 'Five-Star Look' and 'Punjabi Baroque'. Style today represents a mixture of the distillation of the past, interaction with the present nationally and internationally, and the understood need and instinctive desire to look and plan for the future.

Old techniques have become less important. Stone and wood have been joined by steel, glass and concrete, while air conditioning enabled architects to abandon traditional solutions to the problem of ventilation. But today an ever-growing number of architects, interior decorators, and clients are also taking environmental impact into account.

Currently, there is a passionate debate about the degree to which it is acceptable for Indian design to incorporate new global styles. The buzz word for the last few years has been 'fusion': everything has apparently undergone fusion: food, music, fashion and, of course, interiors. On the other hand, Raseel Gujral Ansal, the leading Indian interior designer and decorator, puts her argument against the trend succinctly: 'fusion is confusion'.

One band of designers, however, is celebrating their country's ability to come up with a manner of its own that is commensurate with its cultural heritage and its new-found global preeminence. They are evolving a style which confidently combines the unique wealth of available skills and the realization that it can evolve to provide for today's lifestyle. Here is an explosion of creative energy, pent up and now suddenly unleashed. This is one of the most exciting periods of India's history, as its past positions it ideally to meet its future.

With most houses you have to wait to get a foot in the door before you have any idea of the style and character of the owner. With Adil Iqbal Ahmad, the revelations commence as you step onto the covered front porch of his Delhi house. There you are confronted by a miscellany of Bollywood film posters, classicism in the form of the furniture, ceiling lamps and Kashmiri carpet, a plaster statue of Ganesh, made in a Delhi *busti* or shanty town and bought on the sidewalk there. On the end wall is an immense coloured drawing of the 'tree of life' finished in gold leaf (detail, right), by the contemporary Jaipur artist Osman Bhai – a volcanic explosion of fantastic flowers restrained within a broad gilded frame. The composition of the interior as a whole is precise and well balanced. It's a presentation that leaves you in no doubt that this is someone who is master of his vocation.

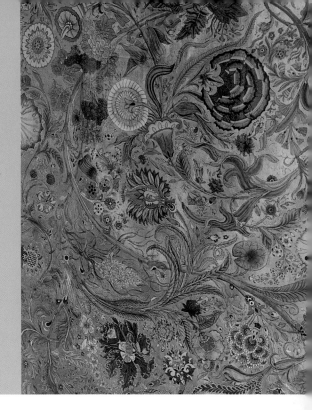

Relief from Lucknow

South Delhi

The citizens of Lucknow, Adil Iqbal Ahmad's home city, were famed as connoisseurs of food, dance, poetry and architecture, ravishing textiles and courtly dress, pigeons, kite-flying, and the cerebral game of chess. Ahmad has inherited this heightened aesthetic sensibility, and his own home reflects his city's rich tradition.

Faced with the global trend towards minimalism, Ahmad does not mince his words. 'I despair of the trend towards what I call the "Hong Kong Airport look." "Died and gone to hell" is how I see it. It is soulless, vacuous and lacking in individuality. So what if the walls are really smooth, the lines perfectly straight – tell me, what else is there to recommend the look?'

Ahmad is very clear as to the style that influences him. The 'comfortably grand informality' of English interiors, he says, 'is what I admire about them – chopped firewood casually stored under a gilt Rococo console topped by a Regency pier mirror. "Shabby Chic" encapsulates the look I love, and grandeur can come in just two rooms, but they have to be chic, they must have a je ne sais quoi about them that is an amalgam of the stylish and classical with a certain gravitas. Above all they must grab your attention.'

below Splendour is not a concept of which Ahmad is shy. 'I am inspired by "OTT" decorators such as Alberto Pinto and Juan Pablo Molyneux, and I love palaces like Blenheim – the scale and opulence, decorated to impress.' And yet 'such grandeur can come in just two rooms, it's simply a question of how you put things together.' Contrived clutter is his signature. The wall hanging is an exquisite piece of *zardozi* (gold thread work), part of a durbar canopy which Ahmad found in the old quarter of Lucknow. The gilt chandelier was designed and manufactured by him. The porcelain on the table was made in China for the export market; Ahmad found it in Hyderabad, his favourite city in India. The glass cabinet and the chairs around the dining table were bought in Pondicherry.

right The black-and-white photographs on the wall are of Ahmad's family, who went on tiger shoots and had vintage cars. (His maternal great-grandfather was educated in England, became the first Indian Chief Justice in British India, was knighted, and was invited by Jinnah to become Pakistan's first Chief Justice.) The chairs are upholstered in an imitation tiger-skin pattern from Italy. The voluptuous cream-coloured bowl is Spanish.

The drawing room is rich with the work of painters, embroiderers, joiners and glass blowers. Each object represents the mastering of a technique and years of acquired skill.

left The coffee table and end tables flanking the sofa were designed by Ahmad and made in his workshops. The two Chinese vases converted into table lamps were bought in Lucknow. On the walls are naïve paintings on glass illustrating the pantheon of Hindu gods, collected in South India, Bengal, and Awadh in the Lucknow region. At the left is a collection of blue glass perfume bottles from Turkey.

left One of Ahmad's most dramatic finds is seen in the entrance hall: a portrait of King George V by Isaac Snowman. The chandelier is from Murano, bought in Delhi. Also bought in Delhi is the antique front door, probably originally used in a mosque. The chair and console table are of the colonial period. The carpet is Kashmiri. Over the door is a plaque from Ahmad's carpet weaver in Kashmir. The small photographs and lithographs are signed portraits of various members of the British Royal family.

opposite In the centre of the room is a glass torchère made in England in the 19th century by Osler of Birmingham, which came out of a palace in Rajasthan. Ahmad's eye as a collector is eclectic. The ceramic mythical birds on the coffee table are from China, the sofa was bought in Pondicherry, the coffee table is contemporary, from Delhi, and the large antique carpet was, like many in the house, made by convicts.

left Ahmad celebrates colour, using it to give
a sense of individuality to each room. The four-
poster in a guest bedroom is a piece from Bengal
of around 1900, as is the figurine of Hindu gods
on the bedside table. The large painting is an
image of Krishna from the town of Nathadwara
in Rajasthan, where there is a centuries-old
tradition of painting such images. The richly
coloured fabrics are all silk-based. The throw on
the bed is an antique sequined *dupatta* (a woman's
scarf); the canopy of the bed is of silk with crystal
glass pendants.

opposite The tablescape in the master bedroom
is as richly eclectic as the rest of the house.
In the centre is a statuette of the flute-playing
Krishna made by the Spanish company Lladró.
Behind it is an unusual vase, a European import
decorated in Art Nouveau style. The curtain fabric
with a Mughal poppy motif is by Brigitte Singh
(pp. 172–79). In the foreground is a Chinese
bowl in *famille rose* style.

'I cannot resist beautiful things, and hunting them down is as much a part of the process as the composing.' On the wall in this upstairs hall are the first 'serious' pieces Ahmad bought, a set of prints of English country houses which he found in Hyderabad. The hanging is one of a pair of fine *zardozi* pieces, which would have been draped on either side of a royal elephant. In the foreground is a handsome Chinese celadon charger, also found in Hyderabad.

left Everything about the house is 'plus size', and many of the artworks were specially commissioned: the painting here is by the renowned contemporary artist Satish Gujral, Raseel Gujral Ansal's father. Most of the furniture is made to order by Casa Paradox, but the iguana-leather-upholstered chaise-longue is by Fendi.

right The family prayer room has a floor finished in marble inlaid with mother-of-pearl, a characteristic signature of Gujral Ansal's, as is her 'cosmic' motif brought into play as the focal point of the room. The dramatic backdrop is gilded with squares of gold leaf.

Chic cool in town

Gurgaon, south Delhi

In the main reception room (*above and opposite*) Gujral Ansal contrasts rich dark wood finishes with tactile-textured and leather cushions (the latter, seen in the foreground in the reflection, by Fendi) and Murano glass, which she loves for its translucence and jewel-like quality and colour. The room, on a scale designed to impress, is divided into two conversation areas. 'I always work to shift one's sense of scale in terms of vision. To suggest my interiors are minimal is to misinterpret my work. With our rich crafts tradition it's all too easy to gild the lily with over-ornamentation. Less is more – but that does not mean minimal.'

Raseel Gujral Ansal and her partner Navin Ansal have created Casa Paradox, a name in interior design and decoration to which India's top industrialists and celebrities must turn when they want a home that is commensurate with their status.

She declines to be drawn on her working method. 'You know, it's like asking for yoghurt to be turned back into milk. There are so many influences that coalesce and evolve into a finished project. I relish opulence, but it should be underplayed: I see the look as wearing an exquisite pair of diamond earrings rather than the whole chandelier!'

As with most of her commissions, she was given carte blanche by her clients, Mr and Mrs Minda, to create an interior that celebrated their success. They wanted a courtyard-style house that was unmistakably contemporary and Western in style, and above all imposing in scale. With instinctive talent and remarkable intuition Gujral Ansal speaks two language styles fluently, that of the West and her own three-thousand-year-old tradition, and here she has fused the two with consummate élan.

opposite

top, left and right At the heart of the house is a spacious double-height room like a covered courtyard or atrium. Here again, Gujral Ansal uses scale to create drama and engage in architectural conversation. She is particularly inspired by the style of Japan – not Zen, but ornamental – and of the region stretching across from there to Tibet: 'there's a certain sensibility of colour which is so distinctive. It is vibrant yet it has a sombre substantive feel.' This appreciation is reflected in the beige and taupe palette chosen for her clients, contrasted with the shimmer of mother-of-pearl and the reflective quality of patent leather.

below, left and right A rigorous masculinity within a given space is always tempered with the judicious introduction of decorative accessories, such as the wholly unexpected pendant light of cut-glass vases ('Cicatrice' by the Italian lighting company Flos) and the soft sheer curtains in the dining room.

right In the entrance lobby, with its massive plate-glass window, ever-changing natural light plays over the surface finishes. 'I am fascinated by the limitless possibilities of textural variety, and the potential to set up contrast and harmony.' Here she has gone for contrast, juxtaposing the smooth metallic quality of chrome with the matt-finished stone walls, and laying an irregular, soft cowhide on the highly polished floor.

'Part of achieving the essence of what I visualized for the interior, a contemporary and occidental concept, meant taking the clients to Milan. I wanted to expose them to the highest international standards.' In the end, she says her inspiration is global, but with an Indian sensibility at the core of any project.

Gujral Ansal seeks fluid space: she is intent that interiors should move seamlessly from one area to another, to avoid any sense that the whole is a series of boxes. And she believes it is possible to mould diverse influences into a cohesive whole: 'culturally rich countries like India can spawn amalgams that are truly evolutionary, and I am confident that India is in the process of an aesthetic evolution.'

In the bedrooms the space is deliberately zoned into three distinctive areas – the bed, floating shelves and desk, and conversation area – maintaining a clear dialectic between the aesthetic and the pragmatic.

opposite, above and below In the bedroom of Mr and Mrs Minda's daughter the strong interplay of cubes is accentuated by the use of youthful colour – light stone and pillar-box red.

above and right The master bedroom displays a muted palette. The strong vertical emphasis of the curtains is set against luxurious indulgence in the details, with contrasting surfaces, sexy sheens, tousled informality, and extravagant mother-of-pearl detailing let into the bedhead.

left Hindu mythology and iconography are key sources of inspiration for Gupta. Here, on a plinth around a *pipal* tree, symbolically sacred in itself, are stone carvings that include a depiction of the goddess Kali set on a capital from a temple and, in the foreground, a stele displaying Shiva's trident, with a niche at the base which serves as a lamp, fed by *ghee* (clarified butter). Marigolds are a traditional offering to the gods.

right The Jade Bedroom. The lamp was devised by Gupta, using an 18th-century wooden column from Kerala. The fabric and cushions on the bed were specially created by India India, a home accessories company run by his wife, Amita Gupta. The pieces are inspired by an antique textile throw from Cambodia, reproduced in a contemporary manner. The drawing entitled *Journey* above the bed is from Gupta's series 'Transformation'.

The art of
contemplation

Gurgaon, south Delhi

Satish Gupta arrived in Paris in 1970 with a scholarship to study art. The atmosphere was still febrile and explosive, a heady mix for an idealistic young man from an upper-middle-class Delhi family. Disgusted by the Vietnam War, he took part in demonstrations in the Latin Quarter and was regularly chased by the French riot police. When not attending class or demonstrating he went busking with an architectural student, Daniel Millet, who played the sitar, and another friend who sang. During his various peregrinations around Paris he came across a second-hand bookshop opposite Notre Dame where he picked up an introduction to Zen philosophy.

From those days in Paris, Daniel Millet went on to become an architect, a lifelong friend, and Gupta's consultant when he came to build this studio and family house. The book on Zen philosophy sparked a lifelong fascination that has influenced both his work and his lifestyle. Today Gupta is considered one of India's leading contemporary artists; a Renaissance man, he is also a writer, poet and sculptor.

'Creating this house was my dream, to create a sculpture that you lived in. I laboured for years on a shoestring budget, one room at a time, to make it the way it is.' Gupta explains his vision of the house as a place that you slowly discover: 'It's like meeting someone new.

opposite The family dining room is kept deliberately austere, with the walls painted a neutral white. Gupta uses this area to display his paintings and sculptures. The table and chairs were designed by him and made by a local blacksmith. The tabletop is of Makrana marble from Rajasthan. The painting, of the goddess Kali, is from his series 'Cosmic Matrix'. The three screens, entitled 'Autumn Forest', are made of iron and brass; the brass leaves – which make a rustling sound in the slightest breeze – represent the *ghee*-fuelled lamps that are lit and floated on the great holy river as an offering to Mother Ganges.

above right A leaf, from an installation centred on a copper Buddha representing the moment of the Buddha's enlightenment.

Gupta repeatedly returned to Rajasthan for
research on his series of paintings of that state,
and this is reflected in the main reception room,
even in the colour chosen for the walls.
As he travelled, he picked up pieces of
architectural salvage and furniture. The traditional
wood-and-rope bed used as a sofa comes from
the nomadic Banjaras, or Indian gypsies, while the
chairs and low table are from the Shekhawati
region in Rajasthan. The cushion covers are tribal
embroidery from Gujarat. Gupta designed the
pot on the left for the New Delhi boutique Prakriti.
The other pots are from Gujarat and would have
been used to store grain or oil. On the wall are
two *pad* paintings from Orissa illustrating stories
of the monkey god Hanuman from the Hindu epic
the *Ramayana*, and a painting on glass of Krishna.

You discover new things about them every time you meet again.'
The various rooms reflect the various phases of Gupta's work, and
the decoration reflects his interests – his love of Rajasthan, his
deep interest in Zen Buddhism and the forms of Buddhism closer
to home in the Himalayan region, and his long-nurtured and finally
realized dream to see the Far East.

The building is clearly divided into two zones, the gallery and
display area and the home. The library serves as both physical
and metaphorical bridge between the two. There is a pervasive
spirituality throughout the house. Gupta does not practise
a religion in a formal manner, but through his work it assumes
a tangible form.

The entrance hall expresses Gupta's interest in
Hinduism and Buddhism. The crushed mulberry
paint is often used to decorate the walls of
Buddhist monasteries in the Himalayas. The
sculptures of mythical lions come from South
India, where they serve as temple guardians.
Capitals from a *haveli* in Rajasthan support them
and also the glazed ceramic amphora, found in
Gujarat and probably used as ballast in the
centuries-old sea trade with East Asia. On the
wall is an old wooden temple from Gujarat, once
used in the prayer room of a private house,
sheltering a brass statue of Garuda from Nepal.
The wall-hanging on the right is a contemporary
tanka from Nepal. At the far left is part of the
exquisitely carved façade of a *haveli* in Pokharan,
Rajasthan, which was being pulled down to be
replaced by a structure in concrete. Gupta bought
the whole building and used pieces from it
throughout his house.

The library is Gupta's inner sanctum, where he retreats to meditate and create. Two walls are covered with serried ranks of books on subjects that range from garden design to metaphysics. Gupta designed the table and chairs and a carpenter made them from local wood. The table, below its plate-glass top, has niches housing objects that Gupta treasures for their arresting aesthetic qualities. On it is a terracotta statue of a monk, next to a granite flower vase by Jivi Sethi and Viki Sardesai's Design Laboratory (p. 90). Gupta improvised the hanging lamp by tucking rice paper under the metal shade to diffuse the light and soften the form.

Behind the table, on the floor, are three antique Kalighat paintings of Shiva. In the centre of the bookcase is a rare *tanka* from Bhutan; below that is a Newari brass *yab-yum* icon of a Buddhist deity with his consort in a Tantric posture, which rests on a Buddhist prayer book wrapped in an orange cloth. On the back wall is a late 19th-century Chinese nobleman's robe, found in Nepal, above a Tibetan chest.

left A breakfast table is laid out amid the lush greenery. In the background is the guesthouse. The vase of flowers on the table, so normal in Europe, is paradoxically exotic in India.

right The family room. The fireplace surround was painted by Khare and reflects Grewal's love of all things ornithological (detail, *opposite*). Above it is a portrait of Khare's aunt; to the left is a print of lilies by the British botanical artist Jenny Jowett. The pair of lamps are made from contemporary milk churns in zinc and iron, painted and gilded by Khare. The large clay pot is Chinese and was used to transport pickles and spices between India and the Far East.

Baronial idyll in a foothills retreat

Dehra Dun, North India

Dehra Dun, in the foothills of the Himalayas, is a welcome escape from Delhi, especially in the summer when the capital's temperature can reach 50 °C. Here Alpana Khare and Bikram Grewal built their new country house on seven acres of hillside that drop down to an ice-cold river over a series of ten broad terraces. The couple are both involved in the international publishing world, have lived in London, and now travel regularly to Europe on business. Grewal is an ornithologist and a passionate gardener; Alpana trained as a graphic designer and is a decorative painter; both are inveterate collectors of antiques. The house had to accommodate a remarkable assemblage of furniture and botanical prints, all in a garden setting.

Their previous house in Dehra Dun had become hemmed in by the town's expansion. Over the years, with a new house in mind, they combed India for architectural salvage and colonial period antiques. In the end they had filled over three warehouses. Says Khare, 'the challenge was to incorporate a vastly disparate collection of antiques and decorative objects. It would turn out to be either a wonderful mix, or a bizarre disaster.'

They named their beautiful family house, in English-style country surroundings, Shaheen Bagh – Falcon's Garden.

opposite Khare and Grewal wanted to create a comfortable, informal house 'for family, friends, the kids, and at least nine dogs, that fitted into its surroundings comfortably and discreetly'. The living area has a baronial feel to it with its double height and a huge library on a gallery that runs round three sides of the hall. The dramatic carved rosewood pediment and columns on the facing wall, bought in Cochin, once framed the entrance to a home in Kerala. The 1930s mirror-fronted bureau on the right was found in one of the junk markets in Delhi. The chandelier is from the palace at Rampur, Uttar Pradesh. The large wooden bracket on the left came from an old Parsi town house in Mumbai. The various pieces of ceramics ranged on the coffee table in the centre of the room were collected over the years during the couple's visits to Spain, France and England. The kilim is from Afghanistan.

The kitchen is usually the most understated area of an Indian house, but Khare and Grewal are bon vivants, and are usually to be seen in the kitchen, often with friends from Europe who are as enthusiastic about food as they. The wall tiles, collected over the years, are a mixture of Chinese, Japanese and British imports, many of them 19th-century. The carved and painted wooden brackets were found in Chennai. Wood and Baroda Green marble from Gujarat are used on the work surfaces.

The one aspect of the new house that Grewal insisted on was a spectacular bathroom. It is divided into two areas by an exquisite lacquer screen depicting cranes, a contemporary piece bought from a departing Japanese diplomat in Delhi.

Featured on the washstand (*left*) is a small part of Khare's extensive collection of enamelware, which was imported into India in the 1930s by the mercantile community of Chettiars in Tamil Nadu. In the background are further examples of Grewal's collection of botanical prints from the late British period. Wherever he goes in the world, he is on the lookout for such analytical prints and paintings of flowers and leaves.

The part of the bathroom with its sumptuous Baroda Green marble sunken bath (*below*) is the one place where Khare yielded to the architect's suggestion to have plate-glass windows. The view is incomparable, onto a small private garden and lotus pond with the hills beyond. From here Grewal may spy in luxury any of the 370-odd species of birds that visit the garden annually. Well before building began he had already planted more than five thousand fruit trees, and created borders and terraces with over a hundred varieties of annuals.

opposite An unusual collection of four-poster beds was assembled chiefly from the Chennai region, which had its own style under the Raj a hundred years ago. Grewal had his carpenter join two single beds sympathetically under a wood lattice canopy. Botanical prints above the bedhead reflect his love of nature.

Much of the detail work commissioned for this house was experimental, such as the double-width front door, which is clad on the outside in woven copper ribbons (see pp. 16–17, 44, 45). The client specifically did not want solid walls on either side of the entrance since this would have made the space dark, so Anastasio hit on the idea of grilles. Since they must not look restrictive when one approached the house, he conceived a series of repeating patterns evoking bamboo.

Air and light in the city

South India

This family home in South India is the result of a tight collaborative effort between the owners, the Mumbai/New York-based international architect Rahul Melotra, and the Italian interior designer and lighting expert Andrea Anastasio.

Melotra was concerned with getting the balance right between the need for privacy in the midst of a busy city and creating an inward-looking space that would be 'as beautiful a world as possible'. The clients rejected air conditioning, preferring the building to work naturally and to enjoy a flexible relationship with the surrounding gardens. Having spent time in Europe, they wanted a house that reflected their international aesthetic, without losing the essence of their own culture and traditions.

Anastasio ingeniously married two of the clients' requirements – their love of openness and light, and of privacy – by transforming security bars into a series of grilles, reminiscent of Mughal pierced stone screens, or *jalis*: their abstract form suggests bamboo, which grows in South India. As a result, the house has a startling lantern effect by night and the feel of dappled light piercing a forest canopy by day. The use of smooth Venetian stucco on the interior walls, echoing an Indian tradition in a contemporary way, is a triumph.

opposite The main public reception area. Rahul Melotra augmented the generous sense of volume in his plan by employing an illusionistic device that avoids any of the public areas being bounded entirely by solid walls: the wall next to the garden is entirely made up of Anastasio's bamboo design, the ironwork mounted on large sliding doors. All the Italian-designed furniture here is low-slung. The 'Donut' easy chairs and sofa, from B&B, assume clear profiles through their dark upholstery. The luminous tables were made to order in India. Together they form strong collages of shapes that transform the pragmatic furnishing into something more like an art installation. The flooring everywhere is Rajasthani marble, easy to maintain and cool to the touch.

below and right A double-height courtyard has been created without sacrificing either light or the free flow of fresh air. The clients wanted a contemporary space that would not encourage over-busy decoration. Within this tranquil envelope, highlights have been created with symbolic and decorative objects that reinforce an Indian essence. Each public area has a remarkable piece of sculpture in stone or bronze: on the left below is a standing Ganesh; elsewhere (right) is a beautiful bronze representing a form of the goddess Saraswati as worshipped in the Jain religion. Thus two distinctive polarities are set up: the international backdrop of Modernism and the focus on Indian high culture. The challenge today, Melotra explains, is to evolve a harmonious pluralism in which both visual vocabularies are simultaneously valued. This, he believes, is the basis for true synthesis and is his indefatigable riposte to the over-used word 'fusion'.

above left Detail of the entrance door, covered with copper ribbons of varying width woven to produce a surface that is alive and tactile.

above right In the staircase hall, the metal poles set at arbitrary angles are an abstract take on tree trunks, complementing the 'bamboo' grilles. The wall is finished with silver leaf.

below left A thin ledge almost vanishes against a band of Venetian stucco, a device used to intensify the ethereal ambience of the interior. On it is a hanging lamp with a figure of Krishna playing the flute, from Kerala, where it provided light in a temple.

below right The 'bamboo' metalwork filters the sunlight by day; seen from outside at night, the effect is of a luminous lantern. The bulbous form of the antique Chinese jar provides a counterpoint to the geometry of the screen and its shadows.

above
The organic geometric theme is established from the moment you arrive at the house. The front door lies in the distance, beyond the drive. In the foreground is an old South Indian vessel known as an *urili*, originally used to cook rice for festivals; every morning fresh frangipani and other flowers from the garden are floated on the water.

top Philippe Starck chairs, discreet and practical, can melt into the background, a quality they share with the vanishing ledges around the house.

above A ground-floor bedroom. The wall above the bed (made in Coimbatore) is covered with wooden strips woven together on site – a warm-textured version of the motif so strikingly applied to the front door (p. 44).

right The dining room. The Italian-designed table, made to order locally, is laid with silver *thalis* (trays), *katoris* (bowls) and beakers. The chairs are by Philippe Starck. The magnificent veined marble is from a quarry in Rajasthan; the brass lamps are from Tamil Nadu.

left An antique lamp from Nair's home state of Kerala serves to float flowers. In temples such lamps, with a rolled cotton wick fuelled by *ghee* (clarified butter), would be lit at dawn and dusk.

right The meditation area, at the highest point of the mansion, where it backs on to the hill. The space is closed on three sides and fronted in the typical way by elegant cusped arches. The deep niches serve as decoration and also for storage. The dado area is simply set off by painted lines, a regular feature in such buildings. The two stools are old Rajasthani pieces; the *charpoy* (wood-and-rope bed) is new, with a Keralan brass oil lamp standing at its end. The bedspread and cushion covers are designed and hand-block-printed by Nair's company, Soma.

A Rajput mansion restored

Jaipur, Rajasthan

opposite The ornate façade of the *haveli*. Much of this attractive frontage had deteriorated to the point of collapse. Nair appointed a full-time stonemason and, using traditional methods and materials, slowly rebuilt it in four stages. Where necessary, new pieces of stone were carved and aged to fit in with the whole – for instance the supports of the *jharoka*, the two-storeyed balcony, which is an essential element of the *haveli* both as decoration and as a viewing platform. Note the *chhajjas*, sloping eaves that project out above the balconies, increasing protection from both the summer sun and monsoon rains.

'If I had ever imagined the extraordinary task of this project I'd have taken fright, run a mile', says Radhakrishnan Nair of his project to resurrect this 19th-century mansion, Ninda Haveli. He adds, 'thank god indeed for foolhardy youth!' Fifteen years on, tenacity, perseverance and a great deal of sang-froid have helped him bring back to life an all-but-lost Rajasthani mansion.

Originally from subtropical Kerala in the far south of India, Nair moved north to the land of desert princes, where today he runs one of India's most successful hand-block-printing labels, Soma. He could also put himself forward now as a structural engineer and a fount of knowledge on the use of traditional building materials.

For years Nair and his Canadian wife camped out to supervise the restoration. The building had laid empty for over fifty years, the ruins stripped bare. Nair is the first to laugh at his initial ignorance and gullibility, as hidden scorpions, both real and in the form of tradespeople, lay in wait along the way to impede progress. 'I have been involved from scratch and it has been a very steep learning curve, but in the end it has been so rewarding.' Nair has not only created a beautiful home, but saved an important piece of architectural heritage.

above In this room Nair had to reconstruct the niches in the back wall. On the floor are traditional white-covered mattresses and bolsters, to which Nair has added scatter cushions covered in one of his company's fabrics. The coffee tables are *urilis*, South Indian rice bowls, topped with plate glass. The standing fan in old-fashioned style was made in Varanasi.

opposite, above In this room restoration work was slow because of the number of scorpions who were nesting here, and a snake charmer had to be called in to draw out a particularly belligerent specimen. The billowing curtain indicates cross-ventilation – a golden rule in all traditional forms of architecture in India. As in most rooms, the jute *dhurrie* on the floor was woven in Jodhpur.

opposite, below The master bedroom, entered through traditional brass-studded double doors. They and the bedside tables were made by a local carpenter. The storage box at the end of the bed was bought in an old furniture shop in Jaipur. The bedspread is a Soma piece. The sari hanging from the ceiling softens the impact of the plain walls.

above Detail of the upper terrace, above the courtyard (*left*). The tablecloth and napkins are from Nair's 'Lotus' collection. From the traditional brass *thalis* vegetarian food will be eaten with the right hand rather than with Western-style knives and forks. This terrace is used in the winter months for entertaining friends at lunchtime, and for much of the year for dinners. An idyllic spot, still, quiet and with a rare sense of isolation, it affords a broad view of the wild hillside beyond, and at night the sky is bright with stars. Nair appreciated the patina on the original wall surfaces, and where repair was essential he chose to live with the contrast of old and new: 'it will weather naturally and in its own way'.

left As with many *havelis* which housed the traditional extended family, Ninda has several internal courtyards; the main ones would have been public, the others used by the family units. And because it is perched on the side of a hill, there are roof terraces on different levels. Nair, always more at home outside than in, has made sure that all these spaces have a relevant use for the various times of day and year. He was determined to save the tree in this particular courtyard because it provides invaluable shade and attracts birds from the surrounding hills. Here he usually takes tea after his daily horse rides, relaxed and away from the demands of his hand-block-printing business in Jaipur.

below and left An al fresco seating area close to the house reflects Patel's Gujarati roots in the low-level seating and simple white covers; the ensemble, particularly the mattresses, is known as *gadda*, and traditionally serves as a sofa, bed and dining chair. At the centre of the table is an old begging bowl. The pair of mythical birds, carved in wood, painted and gilded, are from South India. On the wall are two paintings commissioned by Patel in the 1980s from artists in Tanjore, who maintain the tradition of painting religious art on glass (*left*, Krishna and his consorts). Every morning fresh garlands of marigolds are hung over the pictures as an acknowledgment of the gods they represent.

right A detail of a granite statue of Surya, the sun god, acquired in Mahabalipuram.

Tropical finesse

Alibagh, Maharashtra

Pinakin Patel was born into an extended Gujarati family, the Mafatlalls, one of India's wealthiest cotton-mill owners, and was exposed to Art Deco influences fused with aristocratic Gujarati tastes. His work as an architect and furniture maker, he explains, has evolved with his age and experience. 'I realized that luxury coarsens. It is simplicity that is truly refined, and I began to pare down my style – indeed, all aspects of my life evolved. I noticed the quality of my life rose.' He now firmly holds to the belief that taking less from people, society, or indeed the planet and giving more must be the true way.

Seven years ago he and his wife escaped from Mumbai to Alibagh. Recalling his state of mind prior to the move, he says, 'I was going to lose myself in the concrete jungle. Here I found myself in the forest: the word has a metaphysical connotation, one of its aspects being to turn your back on accumulated aspirations and retreat to the simple life. Living amidst nature, I have rekindled a sense of delight that had been eroded. Nature is always reinventing itself. It provides the core impetus to my architectural and design creativity.'

Patel explains that he is open to international influences, and greatly admires the architects Geoffrey Bawa, Christian Liagre, John Pawson and Ed Tuttle.

above right Close to the raised seating area (*opposite*) is a dining table, which in the subtropical climate of Alibagh can often be used for entertaining. Members of Patel's household arrange the flowers. The china is standard white dinnerware made in Jaipur; the dining chairs are from South-East Asia. In the background, positioned at the four corners of the seating area, are rosewood verandah columns from the Chettinad district, South India. During the day, the tree canopy provides constant shade and animates the area with changing plays of light. Patel is enthusiastic about his natural surroundings and their life-giving forces.

A broad hall runs the length of the house, effectively dividing the residential area from the offices of Patel's architectural and furniture design practice. The stone floor is of 'rough Shahbad', an inexpensive paving material. The desk, of carved rosewood, was made locally in the 1950s; on it stands a sculpture in enamelled copper which Patel acquired in Chennai. The tall vases are Chinese 'sang de boeuf'. At the far end of the hall is a period mahogany console with a marble top.

above The room that combines library and dining room, with a view through to the formal reception space. All the furniture in both rooms was designed and made by Patel and is sold at his store, Pinakin, in Mumbai. The trophy on the dining room table is English silver ('bought and not won'); the small painting is by the Indian artist Sakti Burman, who lives and works in Paris.

right The main reception room is given an almost monastic feel by Patel's use of white and silver at the centre. The painting on the far wall is by Akbar Padamsee, based in Mumbai. The bookstand in the centre is a reproduction of an old piece, while the large bowl near it, of Indian silver plate, is available in Patel's store.

On the domestic front, Pinakin Patel was reintroduced to India and given a fresh insight into subjects that influence design by Dashrath Patel, founder director of the National Institute of Design in Ahmedabad. For his work he will only use artisans. He believes that 'the mechanization, over-organization, distribution and marketing of art and design globally has made the new global style soulless. The need of the hour is to establish a dialogue between the urban shopper in the mall and the craftsman in the village, so that the shopper gets his requirement with hand-touched tactile feelings, and a uniqueness which is impossible in "organized production of merchandise." The craftsman in turn gets to understand how his counterpart in the city lives and functions and what his real needs are, so he is not left to produce mindless kitsch for gullible tourists.'

opposite The master bedroom. Patel's philosophy of simplicity is carried forward in every area of the house. Above the antique rosewood side table is a black on black serigraph by the contemporary Indian artist Akhilesh, who lives in Bhopal. The bed is one of Patel's. Again he has used 'rough Shahbad' paving, which gives a strong unity to the house.

above The painting on the near wall is by the renowned contemporary Indian artist Raza, who has spent most of his working life in Paris. The rice paper collage on the corridor wall is by Yogesh Rawal. The side table is a composite, its base from a foot-pedal-driven sewing machine. The other pieces of furniture were made in Patel's workshops, and are available from his Mumbai showroom.

right A corner of the main reception room. Harmonious balance and arresting forms and images encourage a state of tranquillity. The small painting on the right, where an image of Ganesha is superimposed on a Shiva lingam, is by a young Udaipur artist. The larger work is by Gautam Vaghela, who draws inspiration from the wallpaintings of Gujarat. The armchair is one of Patel's. The trunk is a period piece, and the standard lamp is of alabaster.

left A balcony looking over the garden and swimming pool has the feeling of being hidden up in the trees. No area of the house remains untouched by Pathy's artist eye. The metal foldaway chairs are of a type more usually seen, well worn, at the end of residential driveways, used by night watchmen or chowkidars. To transform them, Pathy commissioned the Madhubani tribal artist Shivan Paswan (see also pp. 62–64).

right Bathing elevated to ceremony. The antique copper tray contains some of the natural cleansing products used by South Indian women – skin scrub, coconut husk, and in the small bowls gram powder, turmeric and roots of the aromatic vetiver plant. The rectangular tray holds purifying scrubbing stones of Indonesian volcanic origin. Behind is the finely carved granite shower base.

Art and seduction in a farmhouse

Coimbatore, Tamil Nadu

Rajshree Pathy is not just a highly successful industrialist, but a women's rights campaigner, an outspoken opinion-former and columnist, a connoisseur, a collector and international proponent of contemporary Indian art, a patron, socialite and world traveller, a member of the swelling band of Indians who are pushing 'India Inc.', sending seismic ripples through global economics. She worked hard to break out of the expectations of her upbringing ('there was never any question that I would have to work'). Today she bears absolutely no rancour about her past: feisty yes, and sexy, and generous to a fault in promoting those around her.

As to the house, Pathy designed it and a civil engineer did the rest. 'I was not about to live in anybody else's idea of a space', she exclaims. 'I can understand other people's love of the opulent, but for myself I want clarity and minimalism.' Her ethos has its pragmatism, as the house also displays her growing collection of contemporary Indian art. 'I've always loved art; it's been my most consistent passion since school days. I bought my first Hussain at the age of sixteen.' Her house reflects her character, not least in its approachability, open on all sides with views onto patios, courtyards, ponds and garden. 'My house has become a revelation of my own inner sense of space.'

below The main entrance to the house has been ravishingly painted with an exuberant depiction of the ten *avatars* or incarnations of Vishnu (see also p. 11). Pathy commissioned three artists from the Chitrakala Academy in Kerala to execute the work; natural pigments were used to produce the luminous colours. On the right, an old bell hangs from thick leather straps. Beyond it is an antique copper *yali* of the kind used to decorate rice barges plying the Kerala backwaters. The paired low seats in the foreground have teak bases overlaid with finely woven wicker mattresses, made in north-eastern India. Free interpretations of lily pads, finished with dyed cement, serve as stepping-stones across the water.

Apart from the front door and a few others, Pathy's house is notable for its lack of barriers, which gives the interior a free-flowing openness. She would say this is a reflection of her own character. Mrinalini Sarabhai, the consummate classical dancer and Independence activist from Ahmedabad, encapsulated that succinctly in a scribble on the wall of the guest bedroom, which ends with a play on Pathy's name, as 'Honoured person of this realm':

> Inhaling take the world with you
> Exhaling give yourself to the world.
> Empty live within yourself:
> Walls are not barriers
> When as yours they circle us with love
> Shree of this Raj.

On the wall at the left is one element of a triptych by the contemporary artist A. Ramachandran, while on the wall ahead is the other half of Balasubramaniam's sculpture, *Introspection* (for the other half, see *opposite*). In the next room, on the floor by the low seat is an antique shell game board. Further on is one of the few doors in the house (characteristically, it is open): inspired by a visit to Murano, the home of Venetian glass, Pathy had it made by setting intense blue glass poles, which she found in an auction room, into a solid dark wood frame.

opposite For a third wall in her house Pathy commissioned the Madhubani artist Shivan Paswan to paint a traditional marriage ritual. The very different murals, unique for a residential interior, showcase the exceptional talent in the region and reflect Pathy's adventurousness. On the pointedly stark white wall is half of an installation by A. Balasubramaniam, a self-image sculpture entitled *Introspection*. The other half appears in the adjoining room (*above*). The low seating in this informal reception area is upholstered in plain white and features a Turkish cushion cover and a pair of cushions covered in textiles from Gujarat and fringed with cowry shells. The silver on the low table is from Rajasthan – an oil lamp, a pair of partridges, and a pair of parrots, the latter a bird synonymous with the Indian landscape, their chatter heard in every park, garden and wilderness.

right The first view of the interior of the house as you walk through the entrance. Set against a wall of glass bricks is a collection of monstrances of Portuguese origin collected by Pathy in Kerala over a period of years. The painted wooden angel came originally from Spain. The brass candle stands would have been used in churches in Kerala. All the pieces are antique.

below A contemporary sculpture by Anita Dubey, part of a series entitled *Wayside Deities*, which is displayed in the dining room (*opposite*), evokes both humour and sexuality. The artist works to provoke dialogue using everyday objects – in this case lavatory pans, red velvet, and steel.

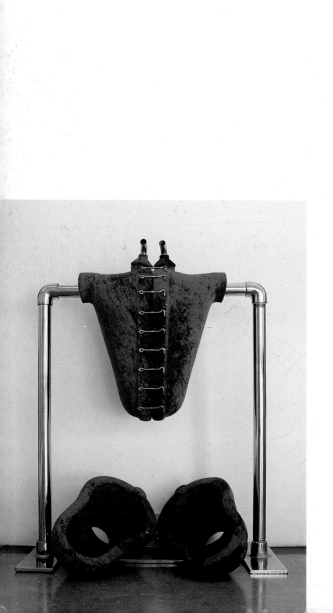

opposite The dining room table, clad in small squares of black mother-of-pearl, was designed by Nirmala Rudhra (see pp. 70–75) and made in Jaipur. The traditional tableware is of silver. The triptych on the facing wall is by Rekha Rodwittya, and on the wall at the right is a sculpture by Anita Dubey (*left*). Drawn to the arts from an early age, Pathy has worked assiduously to sharpen her eye, mature her ideas and explore her own creative strengths, and has spent time with artist friends such as Vasundara and Broota. 'Although I look for perfection, aberration and flaws make life interesting and instil character'; further, she states that 'nothing of beauty can have life if it does not have energy'. She is keen that each of the pieces she has acquired has space to breathe without the distractions of surrounding ephemera.

Pathy's daughter's bedroom continues the sparse
and uncluttered feel of the house, all the better
to showcase art work and furniture. Set on the
Indonesian merbeau wood floor are a cabinet
decorated with a leopard – an original Fornasetti
piece made in 1953 – and a pair of silver-leaf-
covered cubic tables by Nirmala Rudhra (p. 70).
The one in the foreground displays an antique
silver chalice which Pathy acquired in 'Jew Town',
Cochin, and a Venetian blue glass bowl. The
supremely slender bedside lights of steel and
glass are from Fontana Arte.

Rudhra had the original small windows replaced with large expanses of glass to let in more light and enjoy the luxury of the greenery. The sofa, made in Delhi, is a modified version of a classic European type; the side table is a Namboodri Brahmin floor stool from Kerala (see p. 72), mounted on legs. Outside, a small balcony looks over the wall of Humayun's tomb. Here (*left and right*) the cushion fabric is *gyaser*, a heavy brocade from Varanasi. The brass coffee table, which takes its inspiration from the leaves of the frangipani, was designed and cast by Devi Designs, the company of Anupam Poddar (p. 151). The stones that look like Shiva lingams are worn rice-grinding stones found discarded in Tamil Nadu, where Rudhra comes from.

A meditation on scale

New Delhi

opposite The reception area (foreground) and the office. The coffee table set was designed by Rudhra and made in Jaipur, while the cushions are covered with handwoven cloth from Varanasi. A *tanka* from Nepal depicting the goddess Tara hangs above the desk. (For a closer view of the cushions and the objects on the desk, see p. 74.)

Constant curiosity is a way of life for jewelry, furniture and knitware designer Nirmala Rudhra, and she is ever on the move within India and abroad. She travels regularly to Kathmandu in connection with her bespoke knitware and loom-woven Pashmina products, and to Jaipur for her jewelry and furniture work. She considers herself to be a multimedia designer and practises as a consultant for interior design and decoration commissions.

She admits that it was a culture shock migrating to Delhi from her home town of Coimbatore in the South, but she enjoys the spontaneity and social and cultural complexity of the capital. The apartment she found had a wonderful location, next to Humayun's tomb, one of the great works of Muslim architecture, but it was like a corridor. After three years she bought it and immediately commissioned the French architect Stéphane Paumier to rework the space dramatically. The formal reception area, dining area and office zone run down one side of the apartment, while the kitchen area runs down the opposite side and can be hidden behind giant frosted plate-glass sliding doors. Whenever she wants she can wander to a window and stop and stare at the classical beauty of the tomb's dome.

Where the dining area flows into the reception area, dramatic arrangements reflect Rudhra's love of repetition. On the table (which Rudhra designed) is a series of copper and brass ablution vessels from Bengal. On the polished black-marble-fringed shelf, the spiral forms are the prows of traditional rice barges that ply the backwaters of Kerala; beyond are South Indian stone sculptures – a woman from the Pallava period (9th century) and a 10th-century Dakshinamurthi. On the floor are two Namboodri wooden stools in tortoise form, used by Brahmins during temple worship.

above The bedroom is dominated by a Tibetan *tanka* of the Thousand and One Buddhas. The smaller pictures are a set of photographs of Rudhra's mother's hands, taken by her. The standard lamp is classic Noguchi, while the standing lotus is made by Devi Designs (p. 151). The vase is a brass spittoon from Kerala. On the bed is handwoven Varanasi brocade. Standing on the low wall which also serves as the bedhead are two bronze statues of Buddha from Nepal and a brass *stupa* finial.

left Between the seating and desk area a cluster of Tibetan Buddhist statues is joined by a marble lion from Rajasthan and a silver pomegranate. The brocade on the cushions is of a type that has been made in Varanasi for the Tibetan and Nepali market for over three hundred years.

opposite The marble vase was commissioned by Rudhra in Jaipur; its shape is derived from the Mughal metal hookah base. The carvings represent the feet of Jain *Tirthankaras* or saints and are traditionally used in worship.

left Hand-forged brass bowls made up of delicately linked frangipani flowers, by Anupam Poddar's company, Devi Designs (p. 151), are set on a contemporary coffee table whose surface is patterned with rosewood and the semi-precious tiger's eye stone.

right The main public reception room of the joint family house. The coffee tables and low chairs were designed by Saini's practice. The chrome standard lamp is 'Arco', by the Italian lighting company Flos. On the wall is a mixed-medium work by the Mumbai-based artist Smriti Dixit. The Chinese ceramic piece on the sideboard at the end of the room was sourced through an antique dealer in Bangkok.

Sophistication out of town

Chattarpur, south Delhi

opposite First impressions are essential and lasting. Saini's choice of a hand-painted, gold-leaf-finished mural by a tribal artist from the Gond district of Madhya Pradesh is entirely unexpected. It wraps dramatically around the entrance to the Sekhri house. Ideally an interior should also remind you where you are, and the mural does this with precision: India. It provides a link between the essence of the indigenous culture, with its rural bias, and the mores of the influential global movement that much of the rest of the interior reflects.

A chance meeting with Rajeev Sethi in the mid-1990s led Rajiv Saini to abandon his ideas of computer engineering and use his natural inclination for drawing, painting and design in a quite different career: Sethi made Saini the coordinator of a prestigious residential commission in Mumbai – the ideal opportunity for him to learn his trade. In less than a decade, he was recognized as one of India's leading interior designers, with an impressive CV that includes the ground-breaking conversion of a 19th-century fort/palace in Rajasthan into the Devi Garh Hotel, owned by the Poddar family (p. 151) and counted amongst the most stylish hotels in the world.

Here, a mercantile family wanted to transform a house built and styled in the 1980s to accommodate their expanded joint family – the parents and two married sons along with their wives and children. This required common spaces for entertaining, and three separate units each with bedrooms, living room, study and bathrooms. When clients have set out their brief, Saini gives them a masterclass in the possibilities of materials and mediums that can be used, as well as rough drawings of his ideas. 'It's far more exciting if the clients have a clear idea of the possibilities. It's one step at a time, with constant consultation between the two parties.'

opposite Saini uses the words 'beauty' and 'beautiful' when he talks about the interiors of his clients' homes, recalling the French writer Stendhal's observation, 'What we find beautiful is the promise of happiness.' Here he combines luxury (without the flummery often associated with luxury) with the definition of modernity, clean uncluttered forms. The narrow table, designed by Saini's practice, is made of onyx, lit to display the ravishing organic patterns of the stone. The painting, with its views of the human form, is by Jitish Kallat, whose studio is in Mumbai.

right Although a home must serve practically, it can also nurture and enrich the individuals who have consciously chosen and carefully crafted their own environments. A medley of materials is used in the main reception room, from wool and silk to wood, stone and glass, so producing a subtle play of various textures and surfaces. The coffee table and carpet were designed by Saini's practice specially for this space. The sculptures positioned against the facing wall are South-East Asian antiques acquired in Thailand, while the sculpture on the far right is by the senior Delhi-based artist Mrinalini Mukerjee.

below Like his mentor Rajeev Sethi, Saini is aware of the plight of Indian artisans, and also of the extraordinary variety of materials they use, in a huge lexicon of techniques and designs. The sideboard in the joint family dining room displays the technique known as *tar-kashi*, where brass wire is gently hammered into *sheesham*, a variety of rosewood – a craft particular to Uttar Pradesh. The design was composed by Saini's practice after picking several motifs and patterns from the traditional range of designs.

opposite A long wall links the joint-family dining room to the public reception area (p. 79). For practical reasons the two areas had to be divided: Saini used plate glass to preserve the flow of space, and reinforced the illusion of flow by running the long wall shelf through the glass screen. The wall itself is given a parquet effect by a mixture of stone types, treated with a variety of smooth and textured finishes. The surface of the table displays the *tar-kashi* inlay technique (p. 79). On it are traditional silver *thalis* (trays), *katoris* (bowls) and beakers, and brass trivets, based on stylized frangipani leaves, designed and hand-cast by Devi Designs.

right The bedroom/living room combination of one of the sons and his family. The two spaces can be divided by the floor-to-ceiling sliding screen of walnut. The painting in the living area is by the Mumbai-based artist Baiju Parthan. The lights hanging from the ceiling were picked up in the famous Mumbai flea market known as Chor Bazar.

left The bedroom of the senior members of the household is the grandest in scale. It might have been an intimidating space, but Saini has cleverly introduced the effect of a room within a room. The dramatic canopy of the bed is finished in teak, as is the bed base. The pair of sculptures, from a tribal area in the far north-east of the country, were bought from a Delhi dealer. The bedside lights were designed by Philippe Starck and made by Flos.

left The timeless quality of the waterlily, with its rich metaphysical symbolism of purity rising out of murky waters, is contrasted with the luminous acid yellow artifice of acrylic.

right Angularity is the dominant theme, apart from the outstanding Gandhara Buddhist statue with its subtle evocation of draped flowing fabric. The owner explains, 'after a certain stage in life one starts the process of dispensing with visual complication, drawn towards pure form.' The sideboard was made locally to the design of Andrea Anastasio, who also conceived the light box. The lacquer storage jars are contemporary, from Thailand.

Echoed Deco

Coimbatore, Tamil Nadu

opposite The side table and the divan vividly illustrate the Indian industrial community's cosmopolitan sophistication and taste for mixing diverse cultural and period influences. In the divan, made in the 1940s by the Karaikudi furniture company Anjari, Art Deco is assimilated with Hindu sensibilities in the geometric planes of the finial combined with the highly symbolic lotus-flower pendant, and the simple mattress and bolster combination echoes the Hindu minimalist tradition of 'floor living'. On the table is an antique bronze figure of a Jain Tirthankara or saint from Karnataka. The acrylic vase imported from Europe brings the composition vividly up to date, as does the perspex base on which the statue is set. The mirror surface of the table is both new and an acknowledgment of the Art Deco essence of the mansion.

Coimbatore was much like any other agrarian town until a handful of visionaries turned it into one of India's largest industrial mill towns in the latter part of the 19th century; and so it was inevitable that with all that Art Deco stood for – in part a celebration of mechanization – the industrialists of Coimbatore embraced it with gusto when it came into vogue in the 20th century. Mumbai was the most cosmopolitan city at the time, and European architects and furniture companies flocked to the financial hub of the sub-continent. Here the business communities – and Indian princes – were exposed to the machine-age aesthetic. They enthusiastically engaged with it, for it reflected their own forward-looking modernity.

The present owner's father in the 1940s commissioned a Mumbai architectural practice and furniture company to design and furnish his mansion. It reverberated with regular formal dinner and card parties, tended by no fewer than twenty-five retainers. The owner's mother recalls that the one hundred and fifty table-settings were made in Sheffield, each knife and fork so beautifully formed that it balanced perfectly on a finger. Her son remembers that while in the past it was considered inauspicious to buy antiques, she did go

An internal hall illustrates the owner's endeavour to preserve his Art Deco house and at the same time create a contemporary feel. The panelled wood double doors which lead through to one of the numerous reception rooms are original to the house. A construction made of scrap metal from one of the owner's factories serves to screen the staircase. It also creates a niche area for the desk, designed by Anastasio and made locally, and the Philippe Starck chair. Attached to the screen is a striking light installation. Above the desk is an unusual and rare icon once owned by the Mysore royal family, a mixed-medium image of the warrior goddess Durga.

to auction rooms in Ooti to bid for vases and chinaware – but never statuary or jewelry. For his part, he recalls a house constantly full of relatives and their kids, with extra mattresses laid out to accommodate the overflow.

He has had a love–hate relationship with the Art Deco interior of the house, frequently frustrated by the inflexibility of such a defined imposition of the style. All the specially commissioned furniture had its dedicated position in each room, on the pastel-coloured terrazzo floors with their dramatic geometric shapes. The owner

above left In this small reception room built-in cupboards with a blood-red lacquer finish are juxtaposed with frosted glass panels illuminated from behind with an ethereal ice-blue light, evoking Art Deco shapes and effects. The coffee table is original to the house. The armchairs are upholstered in a fabric by the Indian company Atmosphere. The three bronze sculptures (also seen *opposite*) are meditation mirrors associated with the goddess Durga, peculiar to Kerala.

above right A wall of wardrobes sprinkled with silver-leaf lotus motifs was created to make a dressing area outside the master bedroom.

was determined to give the interior a contemporary feel. Equally, he wanted to preserve the Art Deco features, including the terrazzo floors and the covings, should someone subsequently wish to return the mansion to its original state. With the advice of the Italian interior designer and lighting specialist Andrea Anastasio he has effected a sympathetic triumph. Each room in the house has a distinctive colour accent which gives the spaces their own individuality.

left The family dining room has, like the rest of the mansion, been modernized, while carefully retaining the Art Deco features. The walls have been dressed with opaque square panels of glass. On either side of the entrance are exquisite antique silk saris. The table is laid in the traditional way with sets of silver dishes, bowls and beakers. Down the centre of the table is a 'functional sculpture' by the designer Michael Aram (see pp. 104–8).

below Furnished in a thoroughly modern idiom with the exception of the coffee table, which is original to the house, this room has a strong Indian character. The hot pink and flaming saffron are inimitably Indian colours, and the low seating, the swing bench or *hitchka*, and the screen or *jali* at the window are all clear references to tradition. Historically, houses would have had pierced and carved stone screens rather than glazed windows, to allow cross ventilation. Anastasio has designed a contemporary take on that feature with a pierced metal screen which gives the room, obliquely, an industrial feel, and creates an exciting display of light and shadow when the sun shines directly through it.

above On a first-floor balcony the glass brick construction, the aluminium screen pierced with lotus motifs alluding to water (designed by the owner), and the mosquito-screen double doors create the feeling of an installation. But all have a practical application in masking a washstand and the dining room beyond.

opposite In the master bedroom bold stripes in silver leaf run across the matt black cupboards, and their horizontality is echoed by the generous bolsters. The bedposts are machine-finished in aluminium. The floor has a pattern based on an illustration in a book of Art Deco floor designs, executed in colours for which the pigments were imported from France. On the wall are paintings by the artist Raza, who lives in Paris.

left The 1950s chair was rescued from a family storeroom; Sethi is amused by its stiletto legs. On it is a cushion covered with a textile recalling the chintz production in India centuries ago. The fork sculpture, from a Hungarian flea market, was given to Sethi by a friend. The painting on the wall is by Rajit. The fabric reflected in the mirror is a 'Tree of Life' design by Brigitte Singh (p. 171). The table lamp is by Jivi Sethi and Viki Sardesai's company, Design Laboratory.

right The fabrics on the cushions are a mixture of antique and contemporary: the embroidered pieces are antique Gota work from the Punjab, while the quilted piece was designed and made by the Iranian textile artist Sholeh Sadr Sikri. Textiles form a strong theme in the apartment: 'they can do so much for an interior', Sethi says; in India their colours are 'traditionally used to denote the change of seasons, white for summer, reds for winter, yellow for spring.'

Eclecticism and panache

New Delhi

Jivi Sethi epitomizes style and debonair sophistication, but there is a great deal more substance to this design consultant and interior decorator. He's a man of passion who promotes his various causes with equal zeal: one is HIV/AIDS awareness, another the condition of India's craftsmen. 'I am absolutely committed to the extraordinary and diverse craft tradition that India has inherited, in a world that – at the moment – does not appreciate fully what has been handed down to it. I see that the best way for this inheritance to survive the sweeping changes of the modern world is to apply it to the contemporary context.' Through his own work and the Design Laboratory that he set up with his business partner, Viki Sardesai, he is an ambassador for India's artisans.

Sethi describes his apartment as a finished picture built up from a series of pieces in a jigsaw which have been fitted together. 'I love beautiful things and I do believe that however different they may be in style or period, classic or kitsch, they can always work together. I'm a maverick of sorts and my eclectic choices reflect this. My spaces do paint a picture of my personality, my interests and passions, whilst being welcoming and warm. After all, it is my "home".'

right One of the beautiful Kashmir shawls that Sethi has collected over the years.

below 'I forage and buy all the time', says Sethi. The Kashmiri screen is carved with the characteristic maple leaf motif. The daybed is from the colonial period; its mattress is covered in antique *mushru*, a cotton-backed satin fabric made especially for orthodox Muslims who do not wear silk next to the skin, and the cushions are again by Sholeh Sadr Sikri. Sethi loves the contemporary paintings of gods for their kitsch quality. The huge amphora is old, of fired clay, and was used to store grain. The light box tower on the right, commissioned by Sethi, showcases the work of the paper-cutters of Mathura, whose *sanjhi* technique is also used to produce stencils for walls and floors; the motif is of the cyprus tree.

overleaf

left On the side table are temple lamps that Sethi found in Kerala. The handles on the double doors are from Michael Aram's collection (p. 104).

centre The delicate iron doors in the entrance hall were balcony railings, found in a Delhi junkyard and put together in Michael Aram's workshop. The bronze candle stands are Syrian Christian from Kerala, and the test-tube flower vases suspended from the ceiling are by Kavita Datta's home accessories company.

right The centrepiece of the entrance hall is *Transfiguration*, a sculpture in fibreglass and brass by M.J. Enas, a Jesuit priest turned artist. Flanking it are wooden candle stands, Christian pieces from Goa. Old mirrors create momentary vignettes of life as you pass them. The desk is from the colonial period. On the floor are reproductions of old tiles coloured to Sethi's specifications.

left The dining room reflects Sethi's passion for the work of India's extraordinary reservoir of artisans. The black marble plates and beakers, decorated with delicate marble inlay work in Uttar Pradesh and Rajasthan, are from Sethi and Sardesai's company. On the table is a *telia rumal*, a scarf produced by the *ikat* (tie-and-dye) method in village Andhra Pradesh. The torsos on stands are bronzes inspired by tiny originals in gold which Sethi saw in a museum. The *arti* lamps are from Kerala.

below A detail of the table in the anteroom (p. 92). Sethi found the mask of Lord Shiva on one of his frequent visits to Varanasi. The plate is from the 'Sun Pattern' collection by Sethi and Sardesai's company: the technique of metal inlay into metal, known as *bidri*, is particular to the Hyderabad area of Andhra Pradesh. The vegetables, made of wood and gilded, are Balinese.

above One of the apartment's rooftop verandahs. The space is almost entirely furnished with ironwork pieces which Sethi came across in a Delhi flea market. The stained glass panels framed on the facing wall came from a Parsi town house in Mumbai. The set of three bowls on long spider legs is by Michael Aram.

right The charger, by the Design Laboratory, is of black marble inlaid with mother-of-pearl in the form of jasmine flowers. On it stand a *huqqa* base of black marble, also by the Design Laboratory, a leaping leopard in bronze by M.J. Enas, and a piece of red glass of the sort used to make women's bangles.

left Structural work was followed by repair and replastering of exterior and interior walls, and buffing or replacement of the floors. Original architectural detail, such as the striking dados, was preserved and restored wherever possible. In the public reception area distinctively Indian cusped arches spring from finely carved marble columns to form a deep verandah. Flowing water used decoratively is a delicious luxury: light plays on its restless surface, and the sound is accentuated by the echo in this cool hall.

Paradise regained

Samode, Rajasthan

The Rajput rulers of Rajasthan, a land dry, dusty, and in summer unenviably hot, absorbed the ideal of the garden from the Mughals. On the route between their palace at Samode and Jaipur, the Rawals of Samode created an idyllic private garden caravansarai.

Rawal Yadavendra Singh Samode and his wife Arpana Kumari Singh are co-owners of the Samode Palace and Samode Haveli hotels. In the late 1990s they realized what a treasure they had inherited in Samode Bagh (*bagh* means garden). They set about clearing decades of jungly growth to reveal a garden full of magnificent mature trees, and replanted hundreds of rose bushes, pomegranate trees and much more. Finally, they brought back to life the sequence of animated watercourses and fountains that form the backbone of the walled garden.

The garden palace at the heart of the retreat, whose charm lay in its intimate scale, had also fallen into disrepair. While restoring it, the couple found hints of Art Deco and even Neoclassical design in the spare architectural detailing, mixed with Rajput traditions. To complete the transformation, the owners furnished the interior in a contemporary style that reflects their regular visits to Africa, the Far East and Europe.

opposite The concept of a swimming pool is relatively new in the Indian home, where a pool is typically an integral part of the garden, to be enjoyed both physically and visually. Often it also serves as a status symbol, but in more conservative Rajasthan it is incorporated into the private world of the inward-looking *haveli*. Cusped arches supported by marble columns provide an arresting frame around the pool.

right and below The walled gardens are divided by a sequence of watercourses, animated by ninety-one specially commissioned carved stone fountainheads. Planting traditionally includes roses and other scented flowers, and fruit trees such as the life-giving pomegranate. The restored gardens have also become a haven for bird life, including peacocks, the regal symbol of the state.

left Studded doors were recreated and modified to take bevelled glass, to let in plenty of natural light. The black-and-white marble floor in a diamond pattern is surrounded by a border of small white diamonds set in black. The Zanzibar box in front of the window supports an arrangement of pomegranate flowers and fruits.

below A contemporary sculpture of the 'Hand of Buddha'. Like their forebears, Rawal Yadavendra Singh Samode and Arpana Kumari Singh constantly add to the decoration of their palace homes.

opposite The owners wanted to preserve as much as possible of the best architectural detail, but rather than furnishing the house in either 'ethnic' or 'colonial' style they worked towards a clean-cut, international look in keeping with their cosmopolitan lifestyle and outlook.

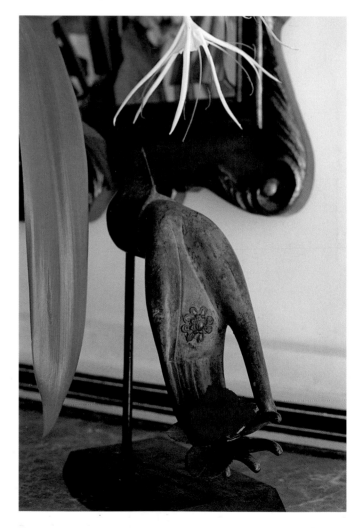

above While the public spaces are contemporary
in style, in the private areas the decoration has
a more period feel. The Singhs' study and television
room is situated next to the master bedroom.
They were keen to preserve the shallow Rajput
relief work on the walls, and the dado (made
of a special plaster almost impossible to reproduce
today) was only delicately cleaned; as in the hall
(p. 98), it is decorated with black tramlines. The
couple wanted this retreat to be snug and intimate.
The wall colour was chosen to be sympathetic
to the wood of the floor, door- and window-frames,
and furniture, and it is also consonant with
the greenery outside. The carpet was acquired
by the couple in Turkey. The photograph top right
is a hand-tinted group portrait of the Rajput
princes before Independence.

above Intimacy rather than ostentation characterizes this guest bedroom. The four-poster bed, from the early 20th century, reflects a combination of British and Rajput princely taste. The painting of a tiger (associated with royal India) was purchased from a local artist working in the Ranthambor tiger sanctuary in Rajasthan. The room gives onto a screened verandah around which the other rooms of the house are ranged.

left The bathroom (perhaps originally a storeroom) has a new mosaic let into the wall. The glass shower screen is framed in wood, warmer and more appealing than metal. The marble floor in the bedroom beyond replaced the original plaster floor, which had not worn well.

Import Export

Since time immemorial India has vigorously engaged in international trade. It is said that the ancient Romans' coffers were bled dry by their lust for Indian fabrics, while in 18th-century Europe Indian textiles became so popular that they were banned. Later, Ahmedabad, 'the Manchester of the East', exported to Europe, to countries around the Arabian Sea, and to South-East Asia: at its height the city supported hundreds of textile mills and employed thousands of people in each.

Today the engagement with international trade has reached new heights. Even as recently as the 1980s few would have predicted that India would challenge the preeminence of the West in global economics and finance, in science, and in research and development.

On a more human scale, India has the world's greatest resource of living crafts to contribute to international art and design. Other countries such as China can reproduce repetitively and mechanically; no country, however, can as India does produce each piece with the individual character of its maker.

India also welcomes artists and designers from across the world, who relish the opportunities that it offers and the wealth of skills handed down from generation to generation. The American designer Michael Aram, who produces his home accessories in India, explains, 'you cannot source the same variety of abilities to produce hand-finished products anywhere else in the world.' Textile designers such as Christopher Moore, from England, feel they are completing a full circle: in India Moore is producing *chinoiserie*, which was so highly sought after centuries ago. The French designer Brigitte Singh is hailed for her exquisitely hand-blocked cotton prints, many inspired by Mughal textiles. Thus Western sensibilities are blended with indigenous talent, creativity and ingenuity, distilled from many hundreds of years of experience.

Equally, a growing number of Indian designers and design company 'names' are establishing themselves internationally with verve and confidence. Not only do they employ hundreds of craftsmen whose skills might have been lost through mechanization, but they are leaders in adapting products made by traditional methods to contemporary use. Anupam Poddar and his creative team at Devi Designs use traditional techniques of brass casting to make products that are relevant to today's local and international markets, and India's top fashion designer, Tarun Tahiliani, harnesses the highly developed and sophisticated tradition of embroidery.

After a period of near extinction, India's artisans have a new lease of life. Their royal patrons may have gone, but the State subsidy that latterly barely maintained them has been replaced by new patrons on a scale that could not have been envisaged: India's growing middle class equals the population of the United States of America, and the world beyond is knocking on India's front door.

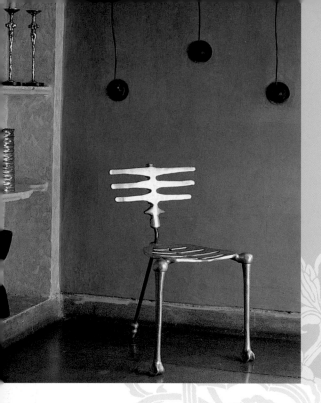

left In designing his 'Skeleton Chair', Michael Aram says, 'I was inspired with the playful idea of sitting on one's skeletal frame.'

right 'Three-Footed Bowls' with 'Neptune' serving set (see p. 108). Much of Aram's work is informed by the natural world, and all of it is hand-forged and hand-finished in India.

An American in Delhi

New Delhi

opposite The entrance hall of Michael Aram's apartment. At this end is a set of metal gates formed from giant bronze keys, wrought in his Delhi workshops. It is both a surreal installation and a witty conceit: a security gate made up of keys. In the centre of the hallway is an exuberant sculpture by G. Ravinder Reddy, entitled *Braid*, an organic blaze of colour inspired by a woman's flower-decorated hair. The chandelier, found in a little junk shop in Delhi, is from the colonial period, which Aram loves; carved flowers and a lotus-topped central column give the piece a botanical theme.

Michael Aram is an Armenian-American designer of cutlery and furniture based in both New York and New Delhi. Since the late 1980s he has produced all his accessories and metal furniture in India. 'Nothing is homogenized in India: every piece has a hand-finished individuality that retains the vibration of the craftsman.'

His apartment was built in the 1940s, when it was still possible to have large rooms. He collects for it slowly and discerningly. 'For me,' he says, 'objects evoke emotion, have rich symbolism and always a strong narrative. So much of what you see is in the mind, all the pieces are brimming with additional meaning and imagery, and it is this which fills the space in the mind's eye.'

Aram laments the contemporary move away from individualism to brand names. 'I want objects that hold mystery, that can be slowly assimilated into a space in the apartment and a space in my psyche.' Speaking of his own work, he says that his raison d'être is to give a decorative twist to essentially practical objects, and that he is fascinated by the ritual aspect of everyday objects such as a spoon or knife. 'I want to produce objects that make you smile, pause and think, and that will enrich and enliven the user's daily ceremony of eating.'

left Leaning against the wall of the living room is an old massage bed from Kerala. Aram says, 'I love it for its simplicity, it is essentially functional but has a strong sculptural feel and is endowed with real soul. I treat it like a work of art'. Before Aram arrived, a single man had occupied the apartment ever since it was built. Every surface was painted in Public Works Department mustard yellow, aged and stained by leaks from countless monsoons. 'It was full of weird relics, receipts strung together on long wires hung from the closets. The flat felt and smelt overwhelmingly musty. I simply wanted to renovate the space rather than change it.' All the doors had been painted, so one of the first jobs he set about was to strip them back to expose the beautiful Burma teak.

below A detail of a tablescape in the living room. The statue of the Virgin and Child was found in South India. The lamp is by a young Indian designer, and the bowl by the artist Nadja Zerunian. The table is covered with the richly embroidered cloth of an umbrella which would have been used in Hindu ritual processions. The fire tongs, entitled 'Vine', embody Aram's fascination with organic shapes and his ability to fuse the practical and the imaginative.

opposite The bedroom is intimate in scale. The focal point is the masculine four-poster bed, possibly a colonial Indo-Dutch piece. The mirror was designed by the American Raphael Serrano and made by Raseel Gujral Ansal's company, Casa Paradox (p. 24). The door handles are 'Eve', one of Aram's casts. He is a great fan of the textiles of Brigitte Singh (pp. 172–79): 'She has made traditional Mughal designs contemporary, transforming their floral motifs into bold graphics, iconic images.' Using dark colours in a lightweight fabric on the windows is a clever device: the dark shades encourage the feeling of intimacy, and the lightest breeze in hot weather causes the cloth to billow, creating a cool ethereal atmosphere.

left Aram brings objects together to form arrestingly composed conversation pieces. Nothing gets lost; each element is able to breathe and yet is part of a coherent whole. He admits to being a workaholic, and his home is very much a part of his work: anything he designs and produces is immediately applied there. Here the standard lamp, table and chair are from the 'Enchanted Forest' collection. On the table are two examples of the 'Three-Footed Bowl' (see p. 104).

below The living room. Aram explains, 'I'm not a rabid consumer but I do like "junking," wandering around Delhi's various junk markets.' He likes nothing more than 'taking nothing and make something, taking a piece that's close to extinction and reviving it'.

opposite The dining area and living area share the same space, but Aram has created two very distinct atmospheres, linked through striking and inspiring objects. The dining area is dominated by two focal points – the end wall, painted an intense sky blue, and the table, designed by Aram. In look the table is monumental and fantastic: a huge slab of rough-edged stone rests on a series of tall cones cast in aluminium in his workshops, some of them gilded. Aram found the metal cut-out of a priest in South India, where it had once been nailed to the exterior of a church as a sort of signboard. The three pictures on the shelves are Raja Ravi Varma oleographs. The 'Vesuvio' wall sconces, bowl and candle stands are from Aram's 'Birch' collection.

left The most striking aspect of Michel and Carol's house is vivid colour. But behind this psychedelic impact there is an underlying thought that combines the visual with the strictly practical. The dyed and polished cement floor is easy to swab down, and the smooth cover on the banquette is quick and easy to clean. 'We try to transform onerous duties into fun activities!' The giant light is an old lamp from an operating theatre, bought in Chennai.

Funk and French irreverence

Pondicherry, Tamil Nadu

'We are the plastic generation and here is the high spirit of Barbie doll in the material world.' Thus Michel Arnaud-Goddet describes his and his wife Carol's house on the outskirts of Pondicherry. The couple, both French, travelled the world and settled on this small city (by Indian standards), falling for its French colonial architecture and the convivial nonchalance of its inhabitants.

The plan was quickly drawn up to produce an easy uncomplicated space. The walls are pure white to catch the light off the Indian Ocean, and the house is arranged practically for living near the sandy beach. The ground floor is given over to the main reception area, including the kitchen-dining space. Two sides open onto verandahs, to ensure cross-ventilation.

'We love the idea of recycling and see wealth in plastic', states Carol. A practising artist, she has performed alchemy on primary-coloured plastic utensils and employs her flair for découpage to rescue furniture others would have discarded long ago. Funky fun is the couple's raison d'être and the 1970s is a period rich in inspiration for them. They celebrate their 'chic and cheap' approach to decoration with gusto. Michel candidly acknowledges that they recognize the children in themselves.

opposite In the small ground-floor bathroom suspended multi-coloured plastic tubs contain all the couple's toiletries, while a snake-like plastic pipe has been transformed into a lamp over the blue-plastic-rimmed mirror. The door is covered in large silver sequins that sparkle like sunlight passing through shallow waters.

below An upstairs room serves as Carol's studio, where she paints. One wall is covered with old Tamil film posters, a passion of Michel's, who says, 'I love the naivety of the themes. They are in effect collages.' Carol not only paints but loves to cover pieces of furniture with magazine cuttings; the stool is an example of her work. The two easy chairs are from the 1970s, re-strung in plastic. The old pedal-driven sewing machine, used by Carol, is protected by an eye-catching plastic cover.

right The raised swimming pool in the walled garden at the back of the house continues the theme of colour, plastic, and fun. A quirky touch of Sixties retro comes from the psychedelic surrealism of the bobbing luminous ice cubes (bought in the local market) and inflatable plastic pillows.

overleaf
Everything in the house is set against immaculate white walls – the light reflected from the sea gives the interior an added luminosity – offset by the audacious and irreverent use of colour. The two white polka-dot-pierced walls (made of cheap cement blocks bought in the local market) screen the verandah against a backdrop of iridescent greens and a firework display of palm fronds. The table, of moulded cement, is surrounded by mass-produced plastic moulded chairs. On it is a South Indian pot, painted with stripes by Carol. The ceiling light was created by Carol from plastic egg-holders.

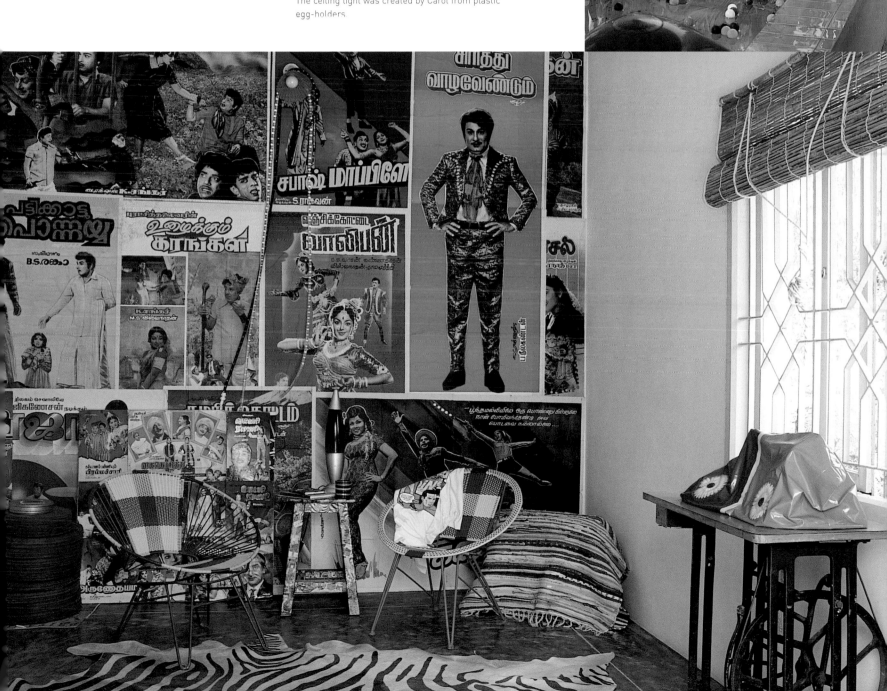

above and left In the kitchen-dining area utensils, bowls and containers from the local bazaar are mixed with Western brand names. A utilitarian strong-box becomes a carefree object after Carol has treated it, and doubles as an outlandishly grand plinth for painted clay figures of Hindu deities. An old Tamil film poster, in itself suggesting exaggerated drama, peers down on the proceedings.

opposite The upstairs landing is lit by a chandelier made of suspended upturned plastic jars bought in the market; coloured plastic scourers tidy up the ends of the steel-tube handrails. The tin trunks too were bought locally. The two paintings are by Carol: 'People immediately assume that my works are based on mandalas. They are not. My paintings are closer to op art. I start in the centre with a small point and turn around it. It gives me a kind of therapy which relaxes me.'

left A moulded plastic Madonna which Arora picked up in Barcelona, Spain, a beautifully crafted toy auto-rickshaw bought in Karachi, Pakistan, and the iconic American cartoon cat, Tom.

right The dining area is set in a deep covered verandah. On the polka-dotted laminated table top in the foreground are three hand-painted plaster statuettes of Hindu deities – Ganesh, Kali and Lakshmi (see p. 119) – which Arora bought in Chandni Chowk in Old Delhi. Beyond, a console table painted a high-gloss pillar-box red stands against a backdrop of broad sky-blue and white horizontal stripes.

Bazaar colour

New Delhi

Think Beatles, think Sergeant Pepper, think of the latter blown so large that the edges disappear – Wham! Think iconic irreverence. Manish Arora's pret-à-porter collections are the equivalent of literary 'stream of consciousness', constant exercises in the experimental, including the mixing of unexpected materials, such as embroidered rexine juxtaposed with traditional silver thread work. It's edgy stuff – funky, brilliantly coloured collages which are sexy, fractious and socially dam-busting. Arora is lobbing grenades of subversion into a world that is already reeling, enthusiastically so, with rampant consumer capitalism.

In the mid-1990s Arora won the Most Creative Student award in Delhi, having devised 'a spoof collection of 16th-century English costumes', and in 1995 his was deemed the most original collection by young Asian designers in Jakarta. In the early 2000s his work continued to meet resistance in certain quarters; but unphased by the naysayers, Arora has since been commissioned by Reebok to create a sneaker collection called 'Fish Fry for Reebok'. At London Fashion Week his collection was hailed by a British designer as 'the most exuberant of the week', and in 2006 he was voted India's top fashion designer by the weekly news magazine *Outlook*.

right 'I guess my house should say that here lives a man who definitely is happy and loves life.' The semi-circular banquette is redolent of a louche nightclub. Although the vertical stripes are as complex as the patterned cushions piled on them, the designs and colours clearly differ, so allowing one to stand out against the other.

below Among the materials in his current ensembles are rexine offcuts, here applied to the walls and the doors and drawers of the sideboard. The almost complete lack of formal furniture is further evidence of just how important the possibility of change is for Arora: floor cushions and bench cushions can be replaced or removed easily. He never spends large amounts of money on furnishings and accessories because it's all temporary and will change – soon and always.

opposite The pearls on the table are from Arora's fashion work. The garland is of the kind used to drape statues of gods in the temple.

right Storage jars of sequins, used on his clothes, provide a constantly changing arrangement. The kites, handmade in their tens of thousands in Ahmedabad, Gujarat, are fleetingly launched into the sky to celebrate the festival of Uttran. The robot toys were found in Barcelona.

right, below Detail of the three plaster statuettes of Hindu deities on the verandah table.

overleaf
left In the small entrance lobby Arora mixes complex imagery and yet produces a clear sense of form. The ceiling is animated by an intricate cat's cradle of fluorescent coloured wool filaments. On the left is a kitsch sculpture from Africa; on the shelf beyond it is a gold plastic revolving candle stand used at Diwali, the Hindu festival of lights. In the zebra-striped shelf unit is an Andy Warhol pastiche – portraits of Arora by an artist friend. The dice stools are common in Delhi furniture markets.

right The four-poster Art Deco bed is the most formal piece of furniture in the apartment, but even it has a kitsch element in the mirror heart at the centre of the bedhead. Arora has used its canopy frame to hang personal trinkets, including his London Fashion Week pass. A knitted toilet-roll cover becomes a hat on a bedpost. The bedcover was bought at Delhi Haat, a handicraft shopping centre, while the rubber dolls above the bedhead come from the flea market in Barcelona. Around the door frames and along the ceiling stencilling is used to produce a lacy edging.

Arora's apartment is consciously impermanent. He moved into it two years ago and finished decorating it in eight days, describing the process as being entirely instinctive, impulsive and without a plan. 'I might change the whole apartment next year. It's the essence of my work – change; it is the driving force, my motivation. My tastes are constantly evolving and I don't want to be stuck with anything that might define my style ten years hence.' For now it is a cornucopia of incongruous 'pop', colour and pattern (he loves Bollywood posters, giant hand-painted film hoardings, and calendar pictures of the Hindu gods). All the fabrics are offcuts from his collections. 'I want people to come here and enjoy themselves. I don't want a house where you have to think twice before you sit, and what's the point of having something that might get ruined.'

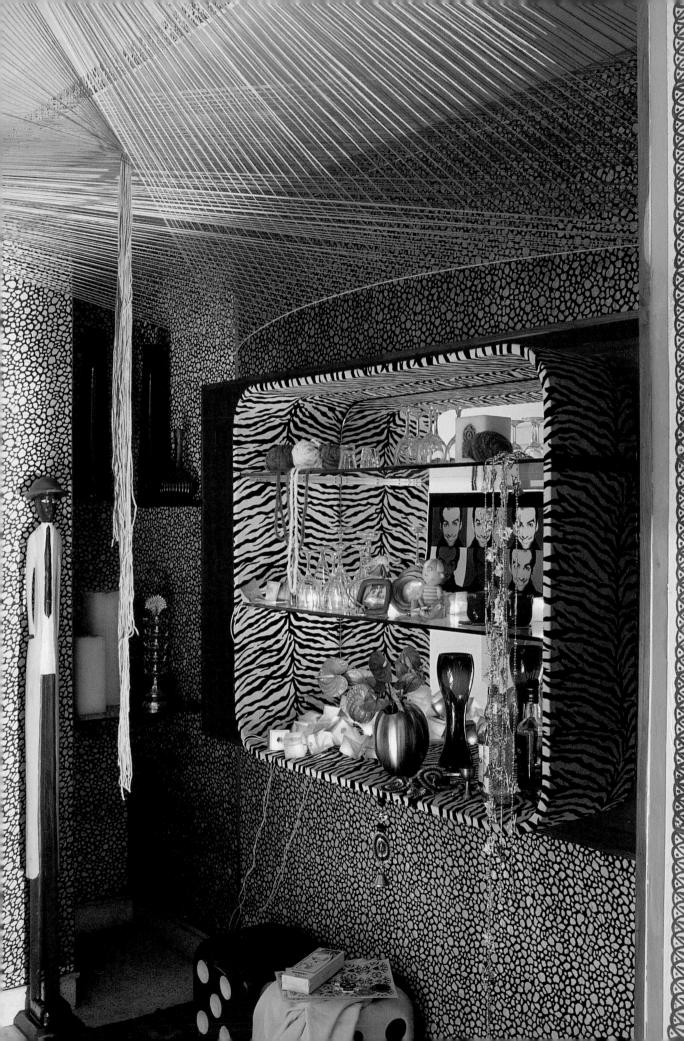

left The painting in the luminous living area is by a friend, Simeen Oshida.

right and below 'I wanted a place that "works", and I wanted to dispense with all the extraneous "stuff" in my life.' In the area designated for visitors (*right*) Merwanji designed an ingenious sliding mechanism to double as the base of the floor-level seat and as a bed. The standard lamp is contemporary, designed by Soto Décor – Sonja Weder and Thomas Schnider – in Goa (see p. 165). The statue, moulded in fibreglass, also appears reflected in the mirror next to the opening that leads through to the other two spaces of the apartment (*below*).

Breeze from the Arabian Sea

Mumbai

opposite Where originally walls stopped the view into the main bedroom, reduced the size of the dining area, and blocked both light and cross-ventilation from the village-side window, now there is a free-flowing space. The louvered doors draw across the two openings when privacy is required. Merwanji bought them in the salvage market for windows and doors in the city. The old cheval mirror and glass-fronted cabinet were found in Chor Bazaar. The large dining table serves both for entertaining and as a workspace. The metal chairs, from the local market, can be quickly folded away to create additional space. The floor is covered with new polished Shahbad limestone, usually used unpolished (compare p. 56).

above right The bathrooms were entirely redesigned and refitted. In the guest bathroom Merwanji enlarged the space so there could be a bath and shower combination. The tribal brass mirror frame is from Madhya Pradesh. The chunky, no-nonsense brass fitments were sourced in the local market.

Suzanne Caplan Merwanji came from Britain and now, married to a Parsi, she lives in Mumbai, where she is involved in one of the world's oldest film industries, Bollywood. Merwanji says she stumbled into this and quickly found she loved it, having to be creative, inventive and resourceful on the hoof. But the hours are often long and demanding, and she decided to leave their rambling Art Deco house for something better suited to her busy life. Concerned friends were doubtful of her choice: it wasn't central enough, too small, dark, a mere collection of characterless cubes. For Merwanji, however, the move was one of her best decisions. She devised a simplified floor plan, transforming three cube-like rooms into a single one to create an open and bright space which can be divided up for privacy when friends and family come to stay. The apartment is now compact, light, easy to maintain, and quick to open up and bring back to life after regular periods when Merwanji has been away on location.

Bandra West, a small coastal fishing village swallowed up by the urban sprawl, has, Merwanji says, managed to retain a strong sense of community. And the apartment enjoys a constant coastal breeze and an incomparable view – a 180-degree panorama of the Arabian Sea fringed by the megalopolis that is Mumbai.

opposite Warm rays of the setting sun bathe the dining table, with cutlery and serving dishes designed by Michael Aram and made in his Delhi workshops (p. 104). The doors temporarily close off the bedroom. The wooden statue was found in Chor Bazaar, as was the glass chandelier, to which Merwanji is slowly adding coloured and clear crystal swags and pendants. She rounded off all the angles where the walls meet the floor and the ceiling. 'This is the first modern building I have lived in. I wanted to take the hard edge off and lose the regularity.'

above The view of the coastline and the Arabian Sea is what Merwanji loves best about the apartment; in fitting new teak windows she subtly narrowed and re-framed the scene. The cushions are covered with *mushru*, a cotton-backed silk fabric worn by orthodox Muslims.

right The main bedroom, seen through the open louvered doors. The lamps are from Soto Décor; behind the one on the right is a painting by Simeen Oshidar. A modern copy of an antique Kashmir shawl lies across the foot of the bed.

left The hall. The painting above the sofa is by Simeen Oshidar. Merwanji commissioned the local carpenter to make the coconut wood coffee table, originally as a bench for the kitchen. The animal figurines are from Madhya Pradesh, made by the ancient lost-wax process. The cushions fringed with cowrie shells were bought in Udaipur, Rajasthan. The wall lights were designed by Merwanji, the wood frames made by the local carpenter and finished by Merwanji with hand-made paper.

right These cushions are covered with a printed fabric, bought in the cloth market in Mumbai, which is used by the local fisherwomen to make up their saris.

India + Portugal + Britain

Nagoa, Goa

Portugal, the former colonial power, engendered a cosmopolitan hybrid in Goa whose liberal way of life and setting with superb white beaches have attracted assorted races for hundreds of years, not least during the heady, hippy days of the 1960s. It is to this social and cultural milieu that Suzanne Caplan Merwanji is drawn, as a relief from her life in Mumbai (pp. 122–25).

The house was in a decrepit state when Merwanji bought it. She relished the challenge, the chance to return it to how it originally was and to mould the space to her own requirements. Once she had cleared it of the various architectural indignities which had been imposed on it – the walling-in of the porch and the division of the main hall into a series of windowless rooms – she was able to give it additional personality, hers. She put in more windows, and louvered doors (the doors and shutters brought from a salvage market in Mumbai), to increase the amount of natural light and improve the views of the garden. Comfort and intimacy are key words, with nothing overly precious, she says. 'Above all, this is somewhere for people, and I want the house to be a pleasure for those in my life with whom I am close, and for the experience always to be enjoyably lazy for my visitors.'

below View from the hall towards the back of the cottage. The Art Deco armchairs were brought from Mumbai. The painting on bone of Krishna is a copy of a picture from Mysore, by a Canadian friend who is a Sanskrit scholar and an artist. Merwanji had a roof constructed over the space beyond, to create a deep-set verandah that protects the area from the sun and also offers an intimate, sheltered vantage point from which to watch and listen to the teeming monsoon rain. The painting on the facing wall was bought at an exhibition of young artists in Mumbai.

right Detail of the coffee table top in the verandah area. The cast bronze hand was bought in Khajuraho when Merwanji was working on location. 'It's made for the tourist market, but I love it anyway.' Around the wrist is a beautifully made bangle from the local flower market. The brass candle holder is a lotus flower which when not in use folds up to become a bud.

opposite 'I'd concluded from frequent holidays in Goa that you rarely used the interior,' Merwanji observed; 'why would you with a climate that is so consistently pleasing, especially in the winter months. I loved the front part of the house, the *balcao* (covered walkway). In the past this is where the owners of the property would sit and chat with any friends who might pass by. But it had been clumsily disfigured, bricked in on either side.' She opened up the views and recreated the generous seating area which leads up to the front door.

above Comfortable informality is the key to the back terrace, with deckchairs and traditional low-slung *charpoys* (rope-strung beds). 'I'm still learning to garden: it's a case of trial and error and reading up in books. Every monsoon things change as I take out plants that haven't thrived and try others.' In the evening the area is delectably sensuous, the garden lit with candles, and candle-laden chandeliers hanging from a tree close by. The air is heady with the scent of nocturnal flowers and heightened levels of ozone from the nearby shoreline, and gently vibrates with the hum of crickets from the forest and paddy fields.

overleaf
left Where possible Merwanji kept the original fixtures and fittings, such as internal doors and floor tiles. The interior has evolved over nine years and goes on changing as she comes across pieces of furniture that appeal. Above the chair are two paintings on glass by Simeen Oshidar which Merwanji particularly treasures.

centre There is an outside shower for bathers coming back from the sea; the internal bathroom is arranged to provide more of the creature comforts. Most of the windows of the house are unglazed but have shutters. For privacy with cross-ventilation Merwanji has installed traditional *chics*, split bamboo blinds.

right These houses were deliberately engineered to provide a retreat from the sun: even here in the kitchen there are high ceilings, which allow air currents to swirl freely, keeping temperatures at an equitable level. The table was made by the local carpenter; the stools were picked up in the local market and painted by Merwanji.

above The bedheads (detail, *right*) were bought
from the design team of Sonja Weder and Thomas
Schnider of Soto Décor (see p. 165). They are
particularly apt as they bear, framed in wrought
ironwork, dried and pressed elephant-ear leaves,
and the plant is found growing in the garden
outside. The bedside table, of coconut wood, was
made by the local carpenter. The prints on the
wall are Indian calendar illustrations by Raja Ravi
Varma. The curtains are sari fabric. The window
grilles were designed by Merwanji and made by
the local blacksmith.

opposite On the wall at the head of the bed is a
patchwork of antique textiles. The painting above
the door is a student work by Manisha Parekh, a
friend of Merwanji, now a respected Indian artist.

left Moving to Bangalore inspired Raj Himatsingka to create her own garden. Through flowers she brings colour into the house with its white walls and wooden floors and window frames. Seen through the window is the main reception area, hinting at the Zen quality of the interior.

right The niche is a ubiquitous architectural detail in India. Raj Himatsingka has turned the form into an installation. The glass vases are filled with sand she collected on travels around the world, including beach sand from Mexico, Positano in Italy, Goa and Puri, transporting her back to distant places. The desert flower arrangement also hints at the purity, cleanliness and simplicity of such environments.

A vanishing act

Bangalore, Karnataka

Raj and Dinesh Himatsinghka moved from Calcutta to Bangalore to start their new company, producing fabrics for the high end of the soft furnishings market in Europe and America. He wanted to use silk as their medium of expression, and the best climate for silk weaving is that of Karnataka, of which Bangalore is the capital (85 per cent of India's silk is produced there). More recently, they took the dramatic decision to open twenty-four chic, contemporary showrooms under the name Atmosphere to showcase their collections.

Over twenty years ago the couple moved as tenants into a house on the site which they always found heavy and oppressive. When the opportunity came to buy the house they immediately moved out and over a two-and-a-half year period comprehensively knocked out the interior and dramatically reconfigured the ground plan. Dinesh – who says he would have been an architect if he had not been so successful with textiles – took a close interest in the design of their new house. The couple knew what they wanted: even before they were married, Raj says, they realized they would always have a common interest in creating the spaces that they would share.

The entrance lobby clearly illustrates the Zen quality of the interior of the house. The sliding panels with their horizontal divisions and frosted-glass finish recall the delicate rice-paper doors used in traditional Japanese homes. The manicured bonsai tree was grown by Raj Himatsingka in the garden.

The house reflects this quiet and unassuming couple. Symmetry always gives a harmonious and balanced feel to an interior; the Bangalore climate allowed the use of mahogany for the floors, softer than the various stone finishes that are frequently employed; and another feature they have used throughout the house is a distinctive type of lighting that gives washes of diffused light.

For them, the acquisition of more furniture or decorative objects is not necessary for the interior to feel individual and complete (see their dining room, pp. 6–7): it already is. 'We are definitely very selective in acquiring "objects." An Italian architect friend of ours once observed that "we are things surrounded by things. Without our knowledge, they affect us." We took this to heart and always think very hard when we buy anything for the house.'

above and opposite, below The Zen flavour, a result of the couple's travels abroad, is, Dinesh Himatsingka says, strongly influenced by Indian tradition combined with contemporary minimalism. The white of the interior, Raj Himatsingka explains, 'is an indeterminate colour, neither cold nor warm. I cannot live with a permanent colour. Colours can accentuate the seasons, blue walls can accentuate a cold day, conversely red walls a hot day'. The drawing room furniture was made by the local carpenter. The horizontal niche (*opposite*) is one of the few decorative features in the room and as a consequence makes a eye-catching statement, all the more so since it takes shape purely by the fall of available light. It is a physical embodiment of the Himatsingkas' quest for calm.

above The upstairs landing is almost entirely free of furniture apart from a working desk and chair. The sitars are not decoration: they were given to Raj Himatsingka by her mother, who taught her to play. The couple have sparingly introduced carpets on the mahogany floors of the house. There are various details that they expressly requested of the architect: the window frames are flat against the plastered walls and have no exposed hardware, and wall edges are softened by the use of grooves.

below The couple's bedroom, with its feeling of spaciousness, is one of the areas of the house they miss most when away on their business travels around the world. Wherever possible, the couple have introduced plate-glass windows so that the garden is a constant backdrop to every room.

opposite Bathrooms are usually the most enclosed areas of a house. The Himatsingkas, however, have taken full advantage of the lush tropical garden outside, which means the room is not overlooked by neighbouring houses. The cupboard doors reflect various influences that inspire the couple – Japanese, with the use of wood, and Indian, recalling the tradition of the openwork screen or *jali*.

left The *trompe l'oeil* in the entrance hall, evoking an arched Ottoman bridge through which the clouds can be seen, was painted by Bronwyn Latif. On the floor is one of a collection of Samarkand carpets. The head of Hygeia is a cast from the National Museum in Athens. Bronwyn had the 'Spanish' wooden table reproduced in Rajasthan.

right Cushions designed by Bronwyn and created in her workshop from silk thread and glass beads on *mushru* (a cotton-backed silk fabric: cf p. 91), edged with ravishing silks that recall the court dress of Ottoman and Mughal noblemen. Her motifs take their cue from the fruits of nature so loved by Muslim artists and their patrons at court.

In the pink

New Delhi

Australian-born Bronwyn Latif and English-born Salim Latif were classic 1970s lotus eaters. They met in London, then decamped to the Greek island of Lesbos for six years, where they were baptized into the Greek Orthodox faith and were married in mid-winter in a tiny church on the side of a mountain. Though both sets of parents clamored for them to settle down, they continued their peripatetic life and travelled overland through Turkey, Iran and Afghanistan, finally arriving in Delhi.

Bronwyn had studied ceramics at the Royal Melbourne Institute of Technology, but never worked in that medium. In Delhi she became fascinated instead by the refined and sophisticated craft of the embroiderers. After a period in couture fashion she opened a workshop producing exquisite embroidery for the soft-furnishing market.

'Oh goodness,' Bronwyn exclaims of the couple's apartment, 'my box, my post-Partition concrete bunker.' But the space provided a blank canvas on which she could superimpose her creativity.

below Almost all the furnishings are second-hand, bought at diplomats' house sales and furniture godowns (warehouses). 'I enjoy the challenge of reinventing a piece.' The shell mirror was created by fixing shells collected on a family holiday at Mahabalipuram to a mirror Bronwyn had picked up in a Delhi flea market. The magnificent screen on the left, which she commissioned, was inspired by one of her favourite places, the dining room of Sultan Ahmet III in the Topkapi Palace, Istanbul. The 'Monsoon Cloud' fabric on the armchair is another design by Bronwyn, inspired by a beautiful breezy room in the Lalgarh Palace in Bikaner. The *mushru* quilted pelmet over the door was suggested by Turkish Iznik tiles and arches. The cane sofa was made to order in Shanker Market, Delhi, from a picture in a book.

right Bronwyn frequently has her leg pulled over her continuing passion for pink. 'No, it's not a joke; actually, it's a kind colour, it's happy, joyful and it's also an Indian colour.' The lotus lights in the foreground, like many fantasy pink objects she has acquired, were found in a Buddhist shop in Sydney, Australia.

She was deeply affected by their travels, she explains, and what she saw provided the core inspiration of her decoration and textile designs. 'My work is predominantly influenced by the visuals I hold in my mind of Asia, the wonderful ceramic tiles. In Afghanistan it was the fabulous Central Asian Russian chintzes – pattern on pattern on pattern. . . . I dream of being minimalist, but I don't think it will ever happen!' She is emphatic about her passion not just for pattern but also for colour: 'The house only works because of colour. Colour is the most important thing in life – probably, that and a bit of frivolity is absolutely essential.'

opposite The dining room is a collage reflecting the Latifs' travels and creative interests, filled with a kaleidoscope of decorative objects that Bronwyn started collecting at the age of fifteen. 'The house only works because of colour, the flow of the interior is to do with the use of it.' She decorated the walls in 'passion pink', wanting the effect of an exploding sherbet bomb. The china on the sideboard comes from all over the world – the 'gardener' from Afghanistan, the Ching kitchen ware from Chor Bazar in Mumbai; the Dutch 'Maastricht ware' was used as ballast on returning ships that sailed to Europe full of spices and textiles. The portrait of Bronwyn was painted in the 1970s by the Australian artist Greg Irvine, who also created the print above the door. The wooden camels on the table may be guardians of the 'protectress of children', who rides across the desert looking for children in distress.

right and below The studio. The Roman blind at the window was inspired by the wisteria Bronwyn was so attracted to in Greece, while the old pastel *dhurrie* on the floor was woven by prisoners in a Rajasthani jail. The Lloyd Loom style chair was made by Manju Singh in Delhi and the lampshade in the corner of the room, with hand-painted images of kingfishers, is from Kashmir. The cardboard cut-out puppets (*below*) were bought by the Latifs' daughter from a street vendor at traffic lights in Delhi late one night. The Rajiv Gandhi lookalike baby doll (*below right*) is a Bala Krishna, probably a processional icon from South India, used during the celebration of Janamastami.

left The bedlinen was embroidered by 'Hoogly-wallahs' in Calcutta, who take their wares round the city piled impossibly high on the back of bicycles, calling out as they move down the streets and lanes and displaying the linens with great ceremony as they unwrap their wares on verandahs. It was embroidery work of this standard that originally caught Bronwyn Latif's eye. The painting over the bed, by an artist in Jaipur, inspired Bronwyn to echo its arches in the room seen through the door. The boxes on top of the armoire are hand-made and decorated with hand-made marbled paper. They store her silk flowers, bangles and party dress paraphernalia.

below The house was built in the 1950s, when it was fashionable for the middle classes to install Western-style bathrooms.

left Samples of Christopher Moore's work are stacked up on a draper's table. Most are variations on *indienne* – 18th-century French copies and versions of imported chintzes produced by the British East India Company in India. The table was reproduced in the local market in Delhi from a photograph of an antique French piece.

right Indigo is one of the vegetable dyes for which India is most famous, and it is a particular favourite of Moore's: 'I've always loved both natural and vegetable dyes, they glow and have a particular luminescence, and it is also the imperfections and the subtle variations of tone and colour which I find so alluring.' Seen here is a selection of historic samples in the Christopher Moore Archive.

Toile and twirl

New Delhi

Christopher Moore was born and brought up in what is now Zimbabwe, and travelled to England in the early 1970s, where he trained as a textile designer (and also as a ballet dancer). He initially specialized in antique French toile de Jouy, and for many years had a shop in London selling textiles he had hunted down in French towns and villages. In 1994 he came to India on an exploratory expedition and saw the potential of the country, and Delhi in particular, for the production of his own textiles; in 2001 he chose Delhi for both design and production. 'I certainly feel more creative when I'm in India. You can have a design idea and have a sample in a day or two. It is the immediacy here, while back in London it can take months to get the same trial.' Toile de Jouy remains a mainstay of his collection, but he has branched out into the designing and printing of indigo and chintz fabrics.

Trade in textiles between Europe and India – chintzes, 'Tree of Life' patterns, *ikat* (tie-and-dye) and indigo – reached its peak in the 16th and 17th centuries, as Europeans succumbed to the printed floral patterns that evolved into the quintessence of English style. Settled in Delhi, Moore feels that he has brought this trade full circle. Most of his work is for the Western market, but he has found that there is now an expanding market in India itself.

right The tablecloth is new, a Rajasthani hand-block-print in an *ikat* design. The small carved wood pavilion is an antique *mandir* or temple, which would have been used in the prayer room of a private house. Next to it is a Kashmiri Cava teapot from the Tibetan market in Janpath. The lampshade uses one of Moore's indigo fabrics, as does the storage box beside the lamp. The grass stool or *mudda* is of a type ubiquitous across northern India.

below Moore calls the facing wall the 'friendship wall' because the paintings are all of, by, or given to him by friends. The *chics* or blinds suspended from the ceiling, made to order, allow the room to be divided up at will. Fabrics on the sofa and chairs are hand-block-prints from Jaipur and Bagru in Rajasthan. The shade on the lamp resting on the draper's table beside the sofa is made from one of Moore's reproductions of an antique Chinoiserie fabric.

left Collecting contemporary Indian art is a serious pursuit for both Lakha Poddar and her son Anupam. It combines many disparate elements; above all, pieces are thought-provoking and arresting – often subversive, sometimes witty. Pop art can also be an ingredient. Here Anupam has brought together hand-painted plaster parrots found in a market in Agra and a refined bowl from Japan. With a strong sense for presentation, Lakha Poddar says, 'you can have couture Issey Miyake with Top Shop: it's the way you bring them together. Only the other day I came across a tradesman selling artificial flowers on the sidewalk. How he had arranged the flowers and their colours was stunning.'

below For their house, the family commissioned the unknown young Indian architect Inni Chatterjee and gave him free rein. Chatterjee was keen to show that when concrete is used innovatively it can be a great building material. The roof perfectly reflects the Poddars' passion for pushing the application of materials and achieving the improbable. Chatterjee wanted to transform this most utilitarian feature into sculpture. The undulations, wrapped in copper, seem detached from the body of the building and evoke waves, the wing of a great bird, or a sari momentarily caught on a breeze. The copper is excitingly juxtaposed with the grey of the concrete. Lakha Poddar says, 'I am happy on any building site. It's the whole process of creation that I love. I love the detail: the foundations, water-proofing, materials, and what you can make them do.'

left Glass bangles have been quirkily adapted and combined with laboratory measuring beakers to make a pair of flower vases. They contrast with the brutalist backdrop of a cement slab wall.

right The bathroom cabinets were designed by Samiir Wheaton, like most of the major pieces of furniture throughout the house. At the outset of the project Wheaton was only twenty-three, and relatively unknown. Immensely creative, he – like the architect, Chatterjee – was invited to come up with ideas, and the finished results are the culmination of discussion, exchange and consensus. The set of rough grey granite vases positioned on the step are a reminder of the type of materials, in their raw form, that have been used throughout the house.

Expect the unexpected

Rajokri, New Delhi

Mother-and-son team Lakha and Anupam Poddar are a formidable duo and undisputed driving force in the nascent contemporary art and design world in India. Through their family's industrial pedigree they have harnessed their influence to campaign with zeal and dedication to showcase the 'new' India, in a way that recalls Charles Saatchi in Britain. Individually, they have specific agendas which they channel through two forums. For Anupam Poddar, there is his company, Devi Designs, which produces hand crafted interior accessories using traditional materials in contemporary designs. For Lakha Poddar, there are her hospitality interests, reflected in the Devi Garh Hotel in Rajasthan, one of the foremost private hotels in the world, noted for its innovative architectural character. If she has a regret it is that she was not able to train as an architect.

Wherever Lakha Poddar travels she finds out what is going on, and she is able to bring to bear her research, along with that of Anupam Poddar, and guide her team in the knowledge that she has always done her homework. Three specific terms define their approach: youth, risk, and indigenous talent. 'Youth is brimming with ideas and a boundless repository of creativity and not inhibited by experience and age', says Lakha Poddar. 'We often go into projects blindfolded. We're told that an idea is too complicated or simply not

The Poddars' activity as patrons of contemporary art is clearly displayed throughout the house, and the exposed concrete and brick finishes provide a flexible backdrop for their paintings and sculptures. Lakha Poddar is aware of the danger of 'wandering in too many directions in regard to collecting', so, she says, 'we have restricted ourselves mostly to collecting works done by Indians, otherwise it dilutes concentration'. The coffee table was designed and made by Samiir Wheaton. Ranged across the top is a set of 'Kamandal' brass vases from Anupam Poddar's company, Devi Designs. The installation on the wall is a piece of street art – a portrait of Mahatma Gandhi on a security shutter, of the type found on town and village shop-fronts, which send out loud reverberations as they are raised and drawn down at the start and finish of the business day.

opposite The entrance hall of Anupam Poddar's zone within a house, which has taken into account the tradition of the extended family home. The area displays the variety of materials used in construction: concrete, wood and stone – and also the family's conscious choice to concentrate on, and thereby encourage, indigenous contemporary arts. The carpet and the painting on the facing wall are both works by the artist S. H. Raza, and running down the wall on the left is a collage of images created by Bharti Kher.

possible. To us, it becomes a challenge. Frequently we are on a
project where we are all "doing it" for the first time. Always we
are resolute about using indigenous talent, from architects
to artisans; we have such an untapped reservoir of talent here that
must be encouraged and spotlighted. What we are trying to create
is a springboard for home-grown talent, to foster an atmosphere
that is forward-looking. We always keep in mind that this is India,
that the work belongs to India and should be done by Indians.
We believe that India has the innate talent, and what matters is the
way you encourage it. Why should we be lagging behind in the
world? That is our greatest challenge – all the time.'

opposite All the spaces in the house are flexible. The astringent mood of the industrial finishes can be transformed through simple additions like the brilliant harlequin screen of loosely draped ribbons and flowers. The long sideboard was designed and made by Samiir Wheaton. The riveted metal overhang which houses a rank of down-lights is similar to a section of aeroplane wing. The decorated cupboard is an old piece from Tibet; on it stand two vases encased in glass bangles (see p. 151).

right The family use the breakfast table in the large kitchen, with lacquer tableware from Burma. The installation ranged against the frosted glass windows is by Bharti Kher. It is the result of an art camp held in a paper factory, where, Anupam Poddar explains, the workers would take off their shirts in summer and hang them on the tree in the compound. One of the strengths of contemporary installation art is its openness to individual interpretation: to some, this may evoke one of Lord Krishna's pranks, when he stole the milkmaids' clothing as they bathed in a pool, and hid it in a nearby tree.

opposite The Poddars have a consummate flair for bringing together disparate concepts, materials and objects, one used to showcase the other. This is perhaps best exemplified in the two large three-sided courtyards, which might have been rather dour due to the limited natural light. Inspired by the glass furniture of the American artist Danny Lane, the Poddars commissioned him to create two monumental glass and water sculptures to sit in the wells. They are a masterstroke. During the day the play of watery green light refracted through the giant slabs of glass and the cascading water bring the courtyards alive. At night, the walls recede into the darkness, and the works transfix the eye with light, movement and sound. The lacquer plates in the foreground are from Vietnam.

above The anteroom displays a large painting by Ramachandran. Samiir Wheaton designed the seating. The lacquer pieces on the coffee table and sofas are from Burma.

right In the small reception room is an artwork by Atul Dodiya (inspired by the logo of the London Underground). The coffee table, of cement, was designed by Anupam Poddar; the silver lotus candle stands on it are products of his company, Devi Designs.

A large flowered Thunbergia grows around the front porch wall. 'I always look forward to getting back to the garden,' says Kinny Sandhu, 'as it has always changed while I have been away.'

The breakfast table in front of the entrance porch is laid every day during the winter months, when it catches the warmth of the early morning light. Kinny says, 'I grew up in the country; I went to school in the Hills and live on a farm. I love the space, colour, fresh air, the country walks and the more congenial way of life country living offers.' The appliquéd tablecloth and embroidered tea-cosy were designed by her and made in her atelier in the grounds of the farm.

Land of plenty and tigers too

Rudrapur, North India

opposite The front porch looks out on the driveway fringed with rose bushes. The colonial period chairs came from Kinny Sandhu's family house. The embroidery on the two side tables was done in her workshops; the wool carpet with chain-stitch embroidery is from Kashmir; and the cushions on the chairs were printed by Christopher Moore in his Delhi silkscreen studio (p. 146). The brass parrot hanging from the ceiling is an oil lamp. On the right-hand wall is a metal frame which is a candle holder, made by tribal blacksmiths in the Bastar district of Madhya Pradesh; such pieces, often placed by the front door as a welcome, were traditionally lit during weddings and to celebrate rituals related to the life cycle.

The Sandhus' farmhouse is set in a belt known as the Tarai (swamp) that runs along the base of the Himalayan foothills, which until the 1950s was wild tiger country, and it has come a long way from its origins as a simple lean-to shed that housed the tractor. Gogi Sandhu is from a Sikh farming family; Kinny Sandhu grew up, she says, 'in a wonderful house in the country in eastern Uttar Pradesh. My mother is Australian and she created a unique style in our home that was a blend of Indian and Western sensibilities.'

Kinny Sandhu has always been professionally involved with textiles. In Rudrapur, where the weavers lived in simple conditions, sleeping in the same room as their pit looms, she built up a workforce of six thousand female quilters, giving them the chance to earn their own money. She set up her own atelier in the grounds of the farm, and from there she runs a bespoke textiles and clothing business.

The Sandhus have spent time away from India, including three years on a farm outside Chicago. But the farmhouse provides an abiding draw for Kinny. 'My preference has always been for a simple colonial style of interior and it is the period on which we have based

opposite The store room is the repository for a growing number of grass, cane and bamboo woven baskets which Kinny has collected in villages on the Plains, in the Hills and in Nepal. What appeals to her in an interior is often not the totality of a look but the detail. 'I'm constantly drawn to a village fruit wallah who has arranged a display of mangoes or placed tiny fresh strawberries in grass basket. Such arrangements inspire me as much as the interior of a grand palace.'

above In the dining room the glass-fronted cupboard, a colonial piece, was picked up in a second-hand market in Delhi. The place mats and napkins were made to Kinny Sandhu's designs by Bengali embroiderers in Delhi. The deer-like animal in the centre of the table is a contemporary bronze from the Bastar district of Madhya Pradesh. The soup bowls on the table are Chinese, bought in Victoria Market in Melbourne, Australia. Kinny admits to a weakness for shopping: 'I am always on the lookout, constantly browsing in second-hand markets, craft fairs, villages, antique shops, boutiques, fabric shops and city markets.'

left Flowers floated in the traditional way in dishes full of water. The vessel at the back is a brass *thali*, of the kind more often used for sorting grains and rice; in the foreground is one of Kinny Sandhu's pieces of blue-and-white china, which she has a particular weakness for and has collected on her various travels to Nepal and Thailand and in second-hand shops in Delhi, Lucknow and Mumbai.

the extensions we have added over the years – large, tall and airy rooms. The most important aspects in my life are my family and friends and it is essential to me that I have a home that they will feel welcome, comfortable and at ease in. My home certainly reflects the things I am interested in: textiles, painting, craft and cooking.' The couple eschewed high-tech air conditioning, which ensures they experience the rhythmic change of the seasons. The verandah and porch are particularly favoured, 'because they allow us to feel as if we are living out of doors most of the year'.

In the master bedroom floral-patterned textiles predominate. The bedspread, which takes its inspiration from Mughal motifs, comes from Jaipur; the carpets, made by Tibetan refugees, were bought in Nepal. The portrait on the wall is of Kinny Sandhu, painted by one of her teachers when she attended the textile school in Delhi. Next to it is a Venetian-style mirror bought in Delhi. The decoy birds on top of the bookcase were made in the village where Kinny grew up in eastern Uttar Pradesh; with hollow bodies, they are designed to serve as boxes for *masala*.

above Another bedroom has ceiling lamps designed by Kinny Sandhu and made in her workshops. The bedlinen, bought in South India, was embroidered in a convent there. Both bedspread and curtains have a traditional ikat pattern. The two generous bunches of scented narcissus in the blue-and-white vases were grown in the garden.

right Kinny Sandhu has always favoured stripes as a decorative form; here she has used them to create an illusion of lofty space in one of the guest bathrooms. The collection of shells is the fruit of beachcombing in Australia and New Zealand on visits to family on her mother's side.

left A corner of Brigitte Singh's garden, set among 17th-century Rajput ruins. On display are two examples of her hand-block-printed fabrics. The wall hanging is one of her most ambitious pieces, inspired by a design she researched in Ahmedabad.

right Niches are ubiquitous in old palace, fort and house interiors throughout Western India (see pp. 50–51), and Brigitte Singh has used this architectural tradition in her new-built home. Tightly arranged collections of small items lend intimacy to an interior – here miniature oil lamps, a model bird from a local market, a pair of tiny brass lamps in the form of human figures holding lamps in their outstretched hands, an old black-and-white photograph of a Rajasthani prince, and shells.

Gallic repose in a *haveli*

Amber, Rajasthan

opposite The view of the garden from the deep verandah is unexpectedly green considering the arid location. The tub chairs, known as *muddas*, are made throughout northern India but particularly in Moradabad. On the pier wall is a metal candle holder made by Bastar tribals in Madhya Pradesh. The table was wrought by a local smith and finished with Jaisalmer stone. The floor is of Kotah stone. An old carpet weight is used as a doorstop. The traditional *chics* are lowered in the afternoon to protect the verandah from the worst of the heat and to dissuade inquisitive monkeys. In the foreground is a bronze *arti*, or ghee-fuelled lamp, from Kerala in South India, very unusually mounted on a wooden pillar.

Visions of Herat, the great mosques of Iran, and the Afghan bazaar were the dreams that filled the mind of the French teenager eager for adventure, recalls Brigitte Singh. She arrived in India in 1980 to study miniature painting in Jaipur, and there she discovered block-printing. Soon she was experimenting – designing and commissioning hand-block-printed scarves and compiling sample books. Today, Brigitte Singh's textiles, unmatched in their exquisitely fine detail, are highly prized in both India and the West.

Singh's output is predominantly floral. 'Much of Islamic fabric design is floral, and I love flowers. Even a few flowers add so much beauty to a space. I need a garden and would not survive without one around me.' The plot of land on which she built her stone house has a set of crumbling, impossibly romantic, ruins which she has worked on to create a garden of Mughal design from which to draw her inspiration. She cites an adage: 'If you want to be happy for a day you have a drink; if you want to be happy for a year you get married; if you want to be happy for a lifetime, work in your garden.'

Singh created her new *haveli* in the early 1990s, inspired by historic models found in Rajasthan which she adores. It is two-storeyed, with

opposite The late afternoon sun filters into the sitting area in the master bedroom, with its storage cupboards. Singh found the colonial ebony sofa in Sri Lanka. The large embroidered cushions and the fine *dhurrie* on the floor come from Afghanistan. The coffee table is made from a wooden stool called a *chokhi*. On the side table under the window is a stack of fabrics bound and wrapped in the traditional way for storage, to protect them from the all-pervasive dust of Rajasthan.

right The kitchen table is covered in a reproduction of a 1780s toile de Jouy. All Singh's fabrics are the result of meticulous research. Apart from the garden, her sources of inspiration are numerous. She pays regular visits to museums both in India and in the West. Antique fabrics, some in private collections and some still to be found in antique shops in the city, provide precious information on colour and dyes. And Indian miniatures offer rich examples of fabrics used in the dress of noble men and women, in awnings and in wall hangings.

overleaf
left The reception room, looking from the living area towards the dining area. The free flowing space was made possible by the use of reinforced steel joists, which freed builders from the structural constraints imposed on houses built of stone and timber. The tiled floor is based on a traditional Mughal design. The coffee table is from Kerala.

centre An Indian-made 1950s two-seater sofa, found by Singh while shopping with her close friend Jivi Sethi in Delhi. The fabrics are from her botanical collection. At the window here, as elsewhere in the room, is a *chic* lined with a fabric of her devising (see also p. 178) which reminds her of the pool where Krishna teased the milkmaids: the central panel was derived from an antique textile in the collection of K. Sangram Singh of Nawalgarh (from whose Indian miniatures, too, Singh has gratefully drawn inspiration), and the lotus border from an old Mughal printed textile in the collection of Hyderabad resident Jagdish Mittal. A papier-mâché bird roosts in the niche.

right On the far side of the reception room stairs lead up to a terrace where, in the right season, kites can be flown. Behind the dining table is a built-in cupboard fronted by wooden doors with images of the goddess Lakshmi, which would originally have been in the *puja* or prayer room of a private residence. In the foreground is one of a pair of late Raj period chairs from the Assembly building in Jaipur, found by Singh discarded on a pavement.

rooms around courtyards. The ground floor is entirely given over to her workshop, while the first floor is her private residence. Singh laughingly says, 'it designed itself rather than me designing it. I love working with traditional builders, people who use such basic tools and yet are capable of such perfection.' She says she is a perfectionist, and that precision is essential. 'I am short-sighted so I have a better view of what's close to me; I have an excellent sense of space, balance and colour. It's genetic.' Singh explains that her grandmother's grandfather was a miniaturist and a textile designer as well. 'I am an incurable romantic, no doubt, and great stories start with dreams.' Much the same could be said of her own work.

opposite

top left The chevron-pattern black-and-white tiles used throughout the reception room.

top right A detail of the kitchen table top, with a toile de Jouy reproduction block print (see p. 175), a vase of flowers from the garden, and a French pewter teapot inherited from Singh's great-grandmother.

bottom left A detail of the iris-patterned curtains in a bedroom (*right*).

bottom right A detail of the composite print behind the 1950s sofa in the reception room (pp. 176–77; see also pp. 102–3). Some of Singh's finest fabrics require as many as twenty-four separate impressions – particularly ambitious since each colour is applied to the cloth with meticulous eye and steady hands. Precision and patience are crucial in the process of hand-block-printing. First, the blocks are soaked in mustard oil, which assists the dyes to sit on the smooth relief surfaces. Next, they are intricately carved. Then, the cloth must be meticulously stretched and pinned on the printing benches. Finally, the blocks are applied in sequence. At the end, Singh herself does the quality control checks

right A bedroom, with curtains from Singh's 'Iris' print collection, inspired by an antique tent print. The bedside table is South Indian. The tiles on the floor were bought locally. Note the papier-mâché hoopoe in the niche above the window. The ceiling light in the background is a period piece which has a mechanism for lowering and raising it. The lamp in the foreground is a reproduction of a traditional type.

left The house forms a shallow crescent round the swimming pool, which assumes an important part of the garden composition and can be viewed from several places indoors. Focal points are provided by the Italianate terracotta pots with dramatic spiky plants.

right The entrance lobby sets the tone of what to expect in the rest of the house. We are met by an explosive arrangement of giant grass that dismisses any concern for the relatively tight space. These grasses are a distinctive feature in the countryside round Delhi and are particularly evocative at dawn and dusk when the sun catches their white manes of seedheads. Larger-than-life red paper poppies bind the whole. The Ming bronze on the table was bought in the flea market in Paris. The pieces of ceramic are by a young Indian artist.

In-between in Sultanpur

New Delhi

opposite For Tahiliani it is essential that you 'always create a mood in which you are going to relax. All too often, Delhi homes have appalling acoustics and hard lighting and huge spaces across which you have to chat.' He describes the drawing room as 'a mad collage of my favourite things and pieces from my travels'. It has the feeling of a French salon: intimate, sensuous and with a tantalizing hint of decadence. Here the focal point is the huge draped curtain. His primary concern in fashion is 'to drape'; the second is 'to embellish'. The painting on the facing wall was commissioned from Chander Bhattacharya. Below it are a lacquer container made by a German living in Chiang Mai, Thailand, and two bell-shaped hookah stands. On the coffee table are various pieces of *bidri*, a pair of maces presented to Tahiliani, and a Tiffany vase.

Tarun Tahiliani, couturier to India's film and television celebrities, is the master of fashion's equivalent of the fugue, multivalent themes fused into a single intricate pattern. And his background? His father was Chief of Naval Staff in Delhi, high representative of the older of the three forces and all that that implies – decorum, discipline, loyalty and deference. 'Life was marked by uniformity, identical houses, identical furniture. You were differentiated by who you were rather than what you had', explains Tahiliani, adding, 'I now see the merits in this system.' It provided a rock-solid foundation.

Architecture was his first love; he studied chemistry and physics at school and went on to one of America's top business colleges, the Wharton School at the University of Pennsylvania. He lived in New York for three years where he completed further studies and ran a small studio. Today in his spare time he is to be found more often than not in front of a canvas, painting.

For his present home Tahiliani made reference to his childhood. He grew up in a Lutyens house in Delhi, with rooms linked by a single large hallway and opening to the garden through verandahs; the high sun in summer could not penetrate, but the low winter sun could.

The brief to the architect here was to create something similar, with a seamless floor, no false ceilings and no cornices, and deep verandahs. The family moved into their new house in 2000.

Tahiliani says that while his essence is Indian, he feels quite as much at ease with Western culture as he does with his own: when you are brought up on Enid Blyton and Shakespeare you are going to be ambidextrous in the way you think and dream. Tahiliani is happy to dip into the cultural reservoirs on either side.

'I want to enjoy the ride, I don't require a five-hundred-million-dollar lifestyle.' He sums up his fashion work as 'a thousand and one ways of embellishment and then simply drape'.

'All the rooms in the house,' Tahiliani says, 'and the dining room in particular, have evolved with my travels.' The dining room is dominated by a crystal and iron chandelier by the Versailles Lighting Company, New York; the table was made for Tahiliani by his 'wonderful' Muslim carpenter, copying an Italian design; the chairs are Iranian; the horn and ostrich-egg wall sconces were bought in Durban, South Africa; the antique mirror came from the palace in Jaisalmer, Rajasthan; and the ornately carved stand at the right, supporting a large vase, is from Gujarat. The colour palette is one that works for him, browns to beige to sand.

Tahiliani has a deep love of the architectural
heritage of India and is angered at how
much of it has been lost, particularly in cities
like Lucknow and Delhi, his own interiors
constitute an ongoing discussion between styles,
periods and cultures. The incidental seating
area in the broad hallway (right) is an example
of this exchange. The large painting on the wall
is an old *pichhavai* (wall-hanging) of Krishna
from Nathadwara in Rajasthan, where there
is a centuries-old tradition of painting such
images. Contrasting with this sacred portrait
is a contemporary sculpture on the coffee table
by the artist Rathore.

Left On the facing wall and at the right are
paintings which Tahiliani has done himself, 'to
have fun and relax'. The sofa is an old monk's
seat from Thailand, carved from a single tree-
trunk. The elephant cushions were brought
back from South Africa. On the floor Tahiliani
has used Shahbad limestone, hand-picked for
its distinctive muddy khaki colour: he explains
that the English, being of a practical nature,
always used this stone to pave their godowns
(warehouses). The mirror on the stand, of wood
inlaid with bone, is new, based on a period piece.

opposite Tahiliani's love of detail and embellishment is reflected in the objects clustered on the table between the two sofas and in the seductive fabrics – faux big cat skin prints on velvet or silk. The tall painting is by him; below it is a portrait of his wife, Sal Tahiliani, by the renowned photographer Prabudho Dasgupta. The lamp suspended from the ceiling on the left is from the flea market in New York; the dark metal Gothic candle stand is from an antique shop in Bangalore, South India; and the standing Buddha visible in the hallway is from Thailand.

above The master bedroom, which looks out on the swimming pool and the garden beyond, is one of the more restrained spaces in the house, with a strong transcontinental influence. The bed, bedside lamps and armchairs all came from New York.

below and right The main reception room. A traditional painting of Krishna from Nathadwara, Rajasthan, hangs unframed on the wall. The floor throughout the house is finished in the same colour, which helps to give a sense of unity and serenity to the whole. 'Attention to such details is often not immediately apparent; however, people definitely feel it even if they don't know it consciously', says Van Damme. She embraces and celebrates the rich decorative arts of her adopted country, deftly mixing sophistication with naïvety, as on the table in the corner (*right*).

left Sensual shapes are used to stimulate the eye. A curvaceous daybed set at the end of a deep verandah gives a 180-degree panorama of the garden and beyond. The situation is equally enjoyable during a torrential monsoon downpour or a winter sunset. The teak pillar is one of dozens commissioned for this courtyard house, carved by woodworkers from Rajasthan. Beyond the pillar, ornamental grasses bring the garden close to the house: Van Damme moved quickly to plant out the garden, to help give the house a settled feel.

right The long deep-set verandah offers an elevated position from which to view the countryside. The roof tiles were hand-formed and baked in wood-fired ovens in Karnataka. Van Damme has given the property a definite European stamp with her choice of colonial style furniture.

Belgium meets Portugal

Bardez, Goa

'Once I start a project, I am very sure. I do things to make them work.' Born in pre-Independence India, Maria Van Damme left when her family returned to Belgium. There she owned a boutique, describing it as a 'little heart of India', and then in her mid-fifties she went to Goa. Soon after arriving, she visited an old Jesuit library in Porvorim. There she came across a piece of writing by a Belgian, Cardinal Suenens, which acted as a catalyst to a life change: 'Happy are those who dream their dreams and are ready to suffer to make them come true.'

'I only like old houses; I never imagined I would build a new one . . . but I bought a plot of land with a wonderful view that includes an ox-bowed creek.' Van Damme wanted the new house to reflect the cultural heritage of Goa and the cross-fertilization of South Indian and Portuguese architecture, and she carefully researched the local architecture, visiting numerous old residences, to find what was most relevant for the climate in Goa. 'Looking at old construction is essential', she says: 'local builders, wherever you are, have always done things for a good reason.' She also wanted a house that drew on the Indian tradition of embellishment but at the same time made a clean contemporary living space, and was luxuriously spacious – an aspect of living too often at a premium in the West.

opposite In a bathroom the pair of mirrors are old and from Rajasthan, while the granite basins were made specially. The deep purple and gold-fringed sari provides a sense of constant airy motion.

above left The formal look of this bedroom is achieved with the colonial four-poster bed, the bedspread pattern with its Mughal antecedents, and the louvered teak doors and fanlight. A painting of Krishna from Nathadwara is positioned against the wall rather than hung upon it. The tousled mosquito net breaks the formality.

above Conjoined views of a bedroom and adjacent bathroom, laid out to allow plenty of diffused light and a constant circulation of air. The bathroom lies beyond the head of the bed, screened by a dividing wall. The only decorative indulgence is the old mirror above the bed, which reflects the verdant exterior.

left In another bathroom, the sense of space is enhanced by washbasins set in marble and supported on a freestanding Victorian base, and the sunken bath.

overleaf The low-set bed is centred to enhance the idea of 'island' and the concept of tranquillity. Nature decorates the walls, as light filters through antique metal *jalis* from Rajasthan.

Acknowledgments

Many people have lent invaluable support and advice in the preparation of this book; in addition to those mentioned, others have been no less generous with their time. Each of you has added to my knowledge and rich experience of India, and I am immensely grateful to you all.

I would particularly like to thank Raseel Gujral Ansal and Navin Ansal of Casa Paradox, Delhi, who over the last fifteen years have given me so much, and more – a home to return to every day, a family, and a reservoir of affection and moral support. Dear Imaan Ansal, their son, never fails to brighten a cloudy day.

I should also like to thank Jivi Sethi and Viki Sardesai for all their encouragement and enthusiasm and for their generosity in giving me valuable contacts.

Warm thanks to Ravi and Uttara Sam, for helping me to keep my feet on the ground and for the most delicious home-cooked food! Thanks too to Nethra and Senthil Kumar, and to Alpana Khare and Bikram Grewal in Delhi.

For their hospitality I should like to thank Suzanne Caplan Merwanji in Bombay; Maharaj Kumar Harshvardhan Singh of Dungarpur and Yuvrani Priyadarshani Kumari of Dungarpur; Kirti Kumari and Maharaj Daivat Singh in Mount Abu; Joerg and Txuku Drechsel of the Malabar House Hotel, Cochin; Sonali Purewal of Zen Space in Delhi; Kinny and Gogi Sandhu in Rudrapur; Bhuvan Kumari at her wonderful guest house, The Cottage, up in Joelikot; and Dimitri Klein and Emilie Thomas at the Dune Eco Hotel, Pondicherry.

Practical thanks to Vicky and Satish Luthra of S.V. Photography, Delhi, for looking after my photographic needs and sourcing film which on occasion proved hard to find in large amounts.

Over the period of twenty-five years if not more I have been continually endebted to those who introduced me to India – Ramesh and Renu Mathur in Oman; Meera, Snehal, Ashish and Aditya Lakhia in Ahmedabad; and Suresh and Rashmi Mathur in Ajmer.

My thanks and acknowledgment to Katherine Morgan, the Vicedirettore of the Milan edition of *Architectural Digest* magazine, who gave me my first break over twenty years ago and who continues to consider my work.

Dr John Snelson has been my greatest supporter in this endeavour. I thank him for his invaluable creative input and his professional editorial skills during my preparation of the text. I should also like to thank my mother and father: this book would never have been completed without their unwavering support.

H. W.
London, 2007